To Ron & Melinda –
Thank _you_ for making our class great!
Please enjoy Melinda!

That's
Entertaining!
WITH TIM LAIRD, AMERICA'S C.E.O.
CHIEF ENTERTAINING OFFICER

Cheers!

SONOMA-CUTRER
ESTATE BOTTLED
2005
SONOMA-CUTRER
SONOMA COAST

WITH TIM LAIRD
AMERICA'S C.E.O.

CHIEF ENTERTAINING OFFICER

PHOTOGRAPHY BY DAN DRY

PUBLISHED BY

BUTLER BOOKS

ISBN 978-1-935497-16-5
Printed in Canada

Photography © 2010 by Dan Dry

Many of the products featured in the recipes in *That's Entertaining!* are registered trademarks.
The authors would like to acknowledge the owners of those products in the following list:

Jack Daniels, Lynchburg Lemonade and Gentleman Jack are registered trademarks of Jack Daniel's.
Southern Comfort is a registered trademark of Southern Comfort.
Canadian Mist, Chambord, el Jimador, Herradura, Pepe Lopez and Woodford Reserve are registered trademarks of Brown-Forman Corporation.
Early Times and Old Forester are registered trademarks of Early Times Distillers Company.
Fetzer, Five Rivers, Jekel and Little Black Dress are registered trademarks of Fetzer Vineyards.
Sonoma-Cutrer is a registered trademark of Sonoma-Cutrer Vineyards.
Finlandia is a registered trademark of Finlandia Vodka Worldwide.
Korbel is a registered trademark.
Tuaca is a registered trademark.
Oaks Lily is a registered trademark of Churchill Downs.
Cholulu Hot Sauce is a registered trademark of Jose Cuervo S.A de C.V.
Tabasco is a registered trademark of McIlhenny Company.
Frank's Red Hot Sauce is a registered trademark of Reckitt Benckiser plc.
Bomb Pop is a registered trademark of Wells Dairy, Inc.
Finest Call is a registered trademark of American Beverage Marketers.
M&M's is a registered trademark of Masterfoods USA.
Butterfinger is a registered trademark of Nestle.
Heath is a registered trademark of Hershey's.
Fritos is a registered trademark of Frito Lay North America, Inc.
Triscuit is a registered trademark of Nabisco and Kraft Foods.
Silpat is a registered trademark of Demarle SA.
Dumante is a registered trademark of Dumante Verdenoce Liqueur.

Book design by Scott Stortz

Published by:

Butler Books
P.O. Box 7311
Louisville, KY 40207
(502) 897–9393
Fax (502) 897–9797

www.butlerbooks.com

*A very special thank you to all of our friends and family
for their inspiration, creative support and enthusiasm
for this project, especially:*

Rick Bubenhofer
Carol Butler
Bonnie Davidson
Virginia Dow
Margaret, Hayden and Meagan Dry
Susie Freydl Carrabes
Meri Chatty Jones
Russell and Charlotte Laird
Michael Lattin
Jim Proudfoot
Sara Stone Psihas
Elizabeth Sawyer
Scott Stortz
The Benzes, Dusas, Eagans, Kipers and LaMontagnes

We particularly would like to acknowledge John Carlos White, publisher,
Food & Dining magazine, for helping to make this collaboration possible.

And lastly, we give a huge heartfelt thank you to our
Brown-Forman family for everyone's support.

Introduction

I have been entertaining for as long as I can remember. My parents love to tell stories of how I always wanted to help with their parties as a very small child. I threw my first dinner party at the age of 12 and have never stopped. Today, my wife Lori and I host almost 50 parties a year because we love getting friends and family together to celebrate holidays, events – anything and everything, really. We have so often met people who really want to gather friends for various events but are intimidated by the thought of having a party. In *That's Entertaining!*, Lori and I share our secrets on how easy it is to entertain at home, and we offer tips on how to get organized so you too can enjoy your own parties.

I guarantee that if you plan ahead and get organized, you can have as much fun as your guests. You will also find that it is economical to entertain at home. You don't have to spend a lot of money to host a festive party with food, fun and flare.

Each chapter in this book is about a special entertaining occasion. We hope you have fun creating your own signature events by picking and choosing different food and drink recipes to build your own party. To get started, here are a few of our favorite entertaining tips:

PARTY PLANNING TIPS

- Decide on a theme, if you are going to have one.
- Put together a playlist of music that either relates to your theme or fits the mood. Cocktail party music can be very different from a formal dinner party. Choose the type that is best for your event.
- Make a list of everything you plan to serve for food and beverages.
- Consider making a signature cocktail for your event.
- Determine the guest list and send invitations.
- Make a detailed shopping list with what needs to be purchased at stores where you shop.
- Make a timeline of activities that includes making a grocery list, as well as listing all prep work leading up to the event – things to do the day before, morning of and hours before, as well as last-minute things before the party. Believe me, this will keep you organized and less stressed, knowing everything has been planned in advance.
- Prepare your table a few days before the party. Take out the serving platters you plan to use and label each with the name of the item it will contain. Determine where each will be placed and set out the necessary serving pieces.
- Make and do as much as possible before the day of the event so you just have to put out the food and drinks, turn on the music, light the candles and be waiting for your guests when they arrive.
- Ask guests to participate by bringing side dishes or helping with coats, cocktails, etc. Everyone enjoys helping and being a part of the party.
- Set up self-serve stations so your guests can help themselves to the bar, appetizers, dessert and coffee.
- Consider giving party favors. It is always nice to leave with a little something to remember a special evening. Place a basket near the door with your party favors in it so you will remember to give them to your guests as they leave.
- Most importantly – enjoy your own party!

Cheers!
Tim

CONTENTS

Tapas Night

Tapas Night

The word "tapas" is derived from the Spanish verb "tapar," which means to cover. Many sources say the original tapas were slices of bread or ham used in Spanish taverns to cover the patrons' glasses of sherry. This was needed to prevent fruit flies from getting in the glass between sips and also gave them something to nibble on while drinking. The word has also become known as a style of dining which includes many small plates for sharing or small bites. A tapas party offers your guests the opportunity to try many different tastes throughout the evening. You can even go beyond the traditional Spanish dishes here and add your own favorite appetizers.

For your tapas extravaganza, plan on making 6 – 8 dishes with 8 portions of food per person per dish. Plan your menu to start with lighter dishes first, then heavier, then dessert or something sweet. Don't forget to offer a traditional Spanish platter with bread, Manchego cheese (a sheep's milk cheese) and Marcona almonds (a shorter, rounder, sweeter almond). Many of these recipes can be used as appetizers for other entertaining occasions.

Several pitchers of Sangria are the perfect idea for your signature cocktail. Alcohol-free versions can easily be made with grape juice, club soda and fresh fruit slices.

Another fun tapas party idea is to have your friends each bring their favorite appetizer or tapas dish to share. Better yet, have them bring one of the following recipes.

Sangria

SWINGING SANGRIA

(This recipe swings as you can use either red or white wine. Merlot for red and chardonnay for white. Try both!)

In a pitcher, add:

1 750-ml bottle merlot

3 ounces Chambord liqueur

3 tablespoons sugar

Juice of 2 oranges

Orange, lemon and lime slices

Chill, and serve over ice with a splash of club soda.

Garnish with fruit slices.

Serves 6 – 8

GREAT WHITE SANGRIA

In a large pitcher or punch bowl, add:

1 750-ml bottle chardonnay

1 liter club soda

2 ounces brandy or Tuaca Italian liqueur

8 ounces orange juice

4 ounces fresh lemon juice

¼ cup of sugar

2 lemons, sliced

2 oranges, sliced

Chill, and serve over ice.

Garnish with fruit slices.

Serves 6 – 8

SPARKLING SANGRIA PUNCH

In a punch bowl or pitcher, add:

2 750-ml bottles Korbel Extra Dry champagne

¼ cup sugar

1 cup brandy

½ cup orange liqueur

Lime, lemon and orange slices

1 pint of raspberries

Chill, and serve over ice.

Garnish with fruit slices.

Serves 8 – 10

Marinated Artichoke Hearts

3 cloves garlic, crushed
⅓ cup olive oil
2 tablespoons fresh dill, finely chopped
2 tablespoons fresh parsley, finely chopped
2 tablespoons fresh basil, finely chopped
2 tablespoons fresh lemon juice

2 14-ounce cans whole artichoke hearts, drained
3 tablespoons red pepper, finely chopped
Salt
Pepper

In a medium-size bowl, combine the garlic, olive oil, dill, parsley, basil and lemon juice. Whisk until well-combined and season with salt and pepper. Add the drained artichoke hearts and red pepper. Mix well and refrigerate for a minimum of 2 hours. Serve cold or at room temperature.

Serves 6 – 8

Tapas Mussels

1 cup chicken broth	1 teaspoon fresh lemon juice
¼ cup white wine	2 tablespoons green onion, finely chopped
2 cloves garlic, crushed	2 tablespoons green pepper, finely chopped
Mussels, 2-pound bag, cleaned	2 tablespoons red pepper, finely chopped
3 tablespoons olive oil	1 tablespoon fresh parsley, finely chopped
2 tablespoons red wine vinegar	Shredded lettuce

In a large pot, add the chicken broth, white wine and garlic. Bring to a boil over high heat. Add the mussels and cover, cook for 6 – 8 minutes until all the mussels have opened, discard any that have cracked shells or are closed. Using a slotted spoon, remove the mussels to a large bowl and, once cooled, pull the cooked mussels from the shells and place in a small bowl. Reserve half of each shell as they will be used to serve the mussels.

In a medium-size bowl, combine the olive oil, red wine vinegar, lemon juice, green onion, green pepper, red pepper and parsley. Toss with the mussels. Spread the shredded lettuce on your serving platter. Spoon one mussel and some of the vinaigrette into each half-shell. Repeat with remaining mussels and shells. Serve immediately.

Serves 6 – 8

NOTE: THE MUSSELS AND VINAIGRETTE CAN BE MADE EARLIER IN THE DAY. KEEP IN SEPARATE BOWLS IN THE REFRIGERATOR. COMBINE AND PLATE JUST BEFORE SERVING.

Serrano Ham Sticks

20 bread sticks
¼ cup honey
10 slices serrano ham or prosciutto

Cut the ham slices in half lengthwise. Brush one end of a breadstick with honey and wrap with a slice of ham. Brush again with honey to seal. Repeat with remaining breadsticks and honey. Serve immediately.

Serves 6 – 8

Baked Asparagus

16 fresh asparagus spears, cut to 3-inch length
¼ teaspoon salt
½ teaspoon black pepper
2 tablespoons finely-grated lemon zest

2 sheets frozen puffed pastry,
   thawed according to package
1 egg yolk
2 teaspoons water
1 tablespoon white sesame seeds

Preheat oven to 400 degrees.

In a pot of boiling water, add the asparagus spears and simmer for 3 minutes. Drop into a bowl of ice water to stop the cooking process and to bring out the green color. On a small plate, mix the salt, pepper and lemon zest. On a floured surface, roll the puffed pastry into a large rectangle. Cut the puffed pastry in 5 x 3-inch rectangles for a total of 8 rectangles (one for each asparagus spear) per sheet. In a small bowl, combine the egg yolk with the water. Brush the edges of the puffed pastry with the egg/water mixture, place an asparagus spear in the center, sprinkle with a little of the salt/pepper/lemon zest mixture and fold in each end of the pastry to enclose the asparagus spear, then roll and seal the end with the tines of a fork. Place the rolls on a lightly-greased baking sheet and sprinkle with sesame seeds. Bake for 7 minutes, rotate the pan and bake for an additional 7 minutes or until golden. Slice in half on the diagonal, and serve warm or at room temperature.

Makes 16

Chickpea Tapas

6 ounces fresh baby spinach leaves
1 16-ounce can chickpeas, drained
1 red pepper, finely chopped
1 tablespoon fresh chives, finely chopped

Juice of 2 lemons
2 tablespoons olive oil
Salt
Pepper

In a large frying pan, sauté the spinach over medium-high heat until just wilted, 3 – 4 minutes. Squeeze dry and chop. In a medium-size bowl, combine the spinach with the chickpeas, red pepper, chives, lemon juice and oil. Add the salt and pepper to taste. Serve at room temperature or refrigerate and serve cold.

Serves 6 – 8

Serrano Ham and Portabella Skewers

24 baby portabella mushrooms, cut in half
1 tablespoon butter
1 tablespoon olive oil
½ cup brandy or sherry
Salt

Fresh ground black pepper
12 thin slices serrano ham or prosciutto,
    cut in half lengthwise
24 short skewers

In a sauté pan, heat the butter and olive oil over medium heat. Add the mushrooms in a single layer and let cook without stirring for 5 minutes. Raise heat to medium-high, remove the pan from the heat and add the brandy or sherry, stir, return the pan to the heat and cook until liquid has been absorbed, about 3 – 5 minutes. Season to taste with salt and pepper.

Skewer one mushroom half, then a slice of ham and, finally, another mushroom half. Continue with remaining mushrooms and ham slices. Serve immediately.

Serves 6 – 8

Fried Olives

1 cup vegetable oil	½ teaspoon garlic powder
30 large green olives, pitted, drained	1 teaspoon ancho chili powder
1 pound Manchego cheese, cut into	2 eggs
small cubes to fit inside the olives	¾ cup panko bread crumbs
¾ cup flour	1 teaspoon black pepper

Heat oil to 350 degrees.

In a small bowl, combine the flour, garlic powder and ancho chili powder. In another small bowl, beat the eggs. In a third small bowl, combine the panko bread crumbs and pepper. Stuff each olive with a cube of cheese. One at a time, roll the olives in the flour mixture, then the eggs and, finally, the bread crumbs. Set aside while the oil heats. When the oil reaches 350 degrees, fry 10 of the olives until golden. Remove to a cooling rack to drain. Repeat with the last two batches of olives. Serve warm or at room temperature.

Serves 6 – 8

Garlic and Brandy Shrimp

2 10-ounce bags of large shrimp, frozen, raw, peeled and deveined	1 tablespoon olive oil
	2 tablespoons brandy
8 cloves garlic, sliced	2 tablespoons parsley, finely chopped
1 tablespoon butter	Salt

Defrost the shrimp according to directions on the package. In a sauté pan over medium-high heat, melt the butter with the olive oil. Add the sliced garlic and shrimp. Cook the shrimp until it turns pink on all sides, approximately 3 minutes. Remove shrimp from the pan and reserve. To the heated pan (off the burner), add the brandy. Place pan back on the burner and stir until brandy and pan drippings reduce, about 2 minutes. Add the shrimp back to the pan, add the parsley and salt to taste. Serve immediately.

Serves 6 – 8

Lima Beans and Sausage

1 tablespoon olive oil	2 10-ounce packages frozen lima beans
1 cup yellow onion, diced	½ cup sherry
2 cloves garlic, crushed	1 tablespoon chopped chives
8 ounces chorizo (pork sausage),	Salt
casing removed	Pepper

In a large sauté pan, heat the oil, onion and garlic. Cook over medium heat until softened, about 3 minutes. Add the chorizo and cook until heated through, about 5 minutes. Add the lima beans and sherry and cook for 5 minutes until the liquid has reduced. Add salt and pepper to taste. Can be made earlier in the day and reheated. Just before serving, sprinkle with chives.

Serves 6 – 8

NOTE: IF YOU CANNOT FIND CHORIZO USE AN ITALIAN SAUSAGE WITHOUT FENNEL SEEDS.

Garlic Chicken

1 pound skinless, boneless chicken breasts,
   cut into 1-inch pieces
½ teaspoon salt
1 tablespoon freshly ground black pepper
1 tablespoon paprika

¼ cup olive oil
6 cloves garlic, sliced
1 teaspoon fresh thyme leaves
½ cup sherry
½ cup chicken broth

Preheat oven to 400 degrees.

In a small bowl, combine the salt, pepper and paprika. Rub this mixture on the chicken pieces and refrigerate until ready to cook. In a large sauté pan, heat the oil over medium heat, add the chicken pieces and cook until browned on both sides, about 6 – 8 minutes (3 – 4 minutes per side). Transfer the chicken to a large baking dish and arrange in a single layer. Return the pan used to cook the chicken to low heat, add the sliced garlic and cook for 2 – 3 minutes, until softened. Add the thyme leaves, sherry and chicken broth, raise the heat to high, and bring to a boil. Pour the sauce over the chicken in the baking dish. Bake the chicken until cooked through, 20 – 25 minutes. Serve immediately.

Serves 4 – 6

Vanilla Custard

This is a traditional dessert recipe served in many Spanish homes and restaurants.

3½ cups whole milk	4 egg yolks, lightly beaten
1 cup sugar	2 cinnamon sticks
2 tablespoons cornstarch	Pinch of salt
6 tablespoons water	Ground cinnamon
1 teaspoon vanilla extract	

In a small bowl, dissolve the cornstarch in the water. In a large saucepan, combine the milk, sugar, dissolved cornstarch, vanilla, egg yolks, cinnamon sticks and salt. Cook over medium-high heat and bring to a boil, stirring constantly until thickened. This should take about 20 minutes. Remove and pour through a strainer to remove any lumps, then pour into dessert cups. Refrigerate for several hours until set. Before serving, sprinkle with cinnamon. Can be made 1 day ahead.

Serves 6 – 8

Timeline

1 WEEK AHEAD
- Shop for non-perishable groceries

2 DAYS AHEAD
- Prepare your table with platters and serving pieces

1 DAY AHEAD
- Shop for last-minute groceries
- Make the Sangrias and slice the fruit for garnishes
- Put the frozen shrimp in the refrigerator to thaw for the Garlic and Brandy Shrimp
- Make the Vanilla Custard; refrigerate until serving

MORNING OF THE PARTY
- Cook the mussels and make the marinade for the Tapas Mussels
- Cook the asparagus for the Baked Asparagus
- Make the Chickpeas Tapas
- Drain the olives and cube the cheese for the Fried Olives
- Clean and cut the chicken for the Garlic Chicken
- Make the Marinated Artichoke Hearts

2 HOURS AHEAD
- Make the Lima Beans and Sausage; refrigerate
- Cook the mushrooms for the Serrano Ham and Portabella Skewers; store at room temperature
- Slice the ham in half for the Serrano Ham Sticks and Serrano Ham and Portabella Skewers

1 HOUR AHEAD
- Make and plate the Fried Olives
- Make and plate the Serrano Ham Sticks
- Finish and plate the Baked Asparagus
- Make and plate the Garlic and Brandy Shrimp
- Make and plate the Garlic Chicken
- Heat and plate the Lima Beans and Sausage
- Finish and plate the Serrano Ham and Portabella Skewers
- Combine and plate the Tapas Mussels

JUST BEFORE THE PARTY
- Set out all food items
- Check bar; fill ice buckets; set out Sangrias

Shopping List

Fresh asparagus spears, 16
Lemons, 3
Frozen puffed pastry,
    2 sheets or 1 package
White sesame seeds
Fresh baby spinach leaves,
    6 ounces
Chickpeas, 1 16-ounce can
Red peppers, 2
Fresh chives, 1 bunch
Green olives, 30, pitted
Panko bread crumbs
Manchego cheese, 1 pound for
    the Fried Olives and 1
    good-size wedge for platter
Marcona almonds
Large shrimp, 2 10-ounce
    bags, frozen, raw, peeled
    and deveined
Garlic, 2 bulbs
Fresh flat-leaf parsley,
    1 bunch
Chicken breasts, 1 pound
    boneless, skinless
Fresh thyme leaves,
    1 bunch
Sherry
Yellow onion, 1
Chorizo (pork sausage)
    or Italian sausage without
    fennel, 8 ounces
Frozen lima beans,
    2 10-ounce packages
Fresh dill, 1 bunch
Fresh basil, 1 bunch
Artichoke hearts,
    2 14-ounce cans
Baby portabella mushrooms, 24
Serrano ham or prosciutto, 22
    thin slices
Bread sticks, 20
White wine
Mussels, 2 pound bag, cleaned
Green onion, 1 bunch
Green pepper, 1
Shredded lettuce, 1 package
Whole milk, ½ gallon
Merlot, 1 750-ml bottle
Chambord liqueur

Oranges, 4 (for sangrias)
Club soda, 2 bottles
Chardonnay, 1 750-ml bottle
Tuaca Italian liqueur
Orange juice, 8 ounces
Lemons, 3 (for sangrias)
Korbel Extra Dry champagne,
    2 750-ml bottles
Brandy
Orange liqueur
Lime, 1
Raspberries, 1 pint

ALSO BUY, IF NOT IN YOUR PANTRY

Unsalted butter
Kosher salt
Black pepper
Olive oil
Eggs
Vegetable oil
Flour
Garlic powder
Ancho chili powder
Brandy
Paprika
Chicken broth
Sugar
Short skewers
Honey
Red wine vinegar
Cornstarch
Vanilla extract
Cinnamon sticks
Ground Cinnamon

Fondue

Fondue

Fondue parties were the rage in the 1960s. Fondue pots and utensils were the top gift-giving items at showers and weddings and for the holidays. I'll bet most households still have a fondue pot somewhere that was handed down or lost in the back of the cabinet. Well, break out the fondue gear, because it is now the rage again. Fondue parties are fun, easy, affordable and great for a crowd.

TIPS ON HOSTING A FONDUE PARTY

1. The number one rule of a fondue party is not to "double-dip." Never double-dip a piece of food or a skewer that has touched your lips or mouth.
2. To avoid double-dipping, make sure you have plenty of wooden skewers so your guests can dip once and discard the skewer. Use olive boats or other vessels to hold the used skewers.
3. Be sure to cut your food to be dipped into bite-size pieces.
4. Have plenty of cocktail napkins available to catch the drips. It is also helpful to have small plates available for your guests to use as their bites cool.
5. Offer a variety of meat, seafood, poultry, vegetables, breads and desserts to meet your guests' dietary needs.
6. For larger parties, you can set up fondue stations such as appetizers, entrées and desserts.
7. Have your fondues mainly as warm dips. This way, you don't have to worry about cooking meat to a specific temperature.
8. If a man drops a piece of food in the fondue pot, he is supposed to buy a bottle of wine for the hosts or the table. If a woman drops a piece of food in the pot, she is supposed to kiss the person to her left. Be careful who is standing next to you at a fondue party!
9. If you do not own a fondue pot, borrow one from a friend, have your guests bring theirs, or just use a small chafing dish.

HISTORY

Swiss peasants needed a way to eat their hardened cheese and dried bread so they set up a communal pot over a low fire to melt the cheese and dip their bread. During the 1950s there was a drop in the cheese industry in Switzerland, so fondue was promoted to boost sales. It became popular in the United States in the 1960s as tourists discovered it abroad and began trying it at home upon their return.

The word "fondue" comes from the French verb "fondre," meaning to melt.

FONDUE

Brie and Wild Mushroom with Vegetables

1 ounce dried porcini mushrooms	2 tablespoons cornstarch
3 tablespoons unsalted butter	1 cup chardonnay
8 ounces fresh shiitake mushrooms, stems removed, chopped	1 baguette, cut into 1-inch cubes
3 tablespoons shallots, chopped	2 bunches asparagus
1 pound wheel of Brie, cold, rind removed and cut into ½-inch pieces	2 pounds red skin potatoes
	Salt
	Pepper

FOR THE FONDUE

Bring 1 cup water to a boil in a small saucepan. Add the porcini mushrooms, remove from the heat and let stand for 20 minutes until the mushrooms are softened. Using a slotted spoon, transfer the mushrooms to a cutting board and chop coarsely. Reserve the soaking liquid.

In a large saucepan over medium heat, melt the butter. Add the shiitake mushrooms and sauté until tender, about 4 minutes. Add the shallots and sauté 1 minute. Add the porcini-soaking liquid, making sure not to add any of the sediment in the bottom of the pan. Simmer until liquid evaporates, about 5 minutes.

Toss the Brie with cornstarch in a large bowl until all the pieces are well-coated. Add the chardonnay to the mushroom mixture and bring to a simmer over medium heat. Add the Brie to the mushroom mixture in 3 batches, whisking after each batch, making sure it is melted before adding more. Continue whisking until the mixture is smooth and just begins to simmer. Do not boil. Season to taste with salt and pepper. Transfer the mixture to a fondue pot or pan on a portable burner for serving. Serve with bread, asparagus spears and red skin potatoes.

FOR THE ASPARAGUS
2 bunches asparagus

Prepare a large bowl of cold water with ice. Pour 1 inch of tap water into a large frying pan and bring to a boil. Add the asparagus, return to a boil, and cook until the asparagus is bright green and just tender, about 2 minutes. Plunge the asparagus into the cold water to stop the cooking process. When cool, drain well and pat dry. Refrigerate until ready to serve.

FOR THE RED SKIN POTATOES
2 pounds red skin potatoes, cut into 1-inch cubes
1 quart water
Salt
Pepper

In a medium-size pan, bring the water to a boil. Add the potatoes and simmer until fork-tender, about 12 minutes. Drain, toss with salt and pepper. Store at room temperature until ready to serve.

Serves 6 – 8

NOTE: TO MAKE ASPARAGUS MORE TENDER, BREAK OFF THE WOODY STEMS AND PEEL, USING A VEGETABLE PEELER TO EXPOSE THE BOTTOM HALF OF THE SPEAR. BE CAREFUL NOT TO OVERCOOK THE ASPARAGUS, AS THE SPEARS WILL BECOME LIMP AND DIFFICULT TO PICK UP AND DIP IN THE FONDUE.

Barbecue with Chicken, Pork and Turkey Meatballs

FOR THE FONDUE

1 28-ounce bottle Jack Daniel's Barbecue Sauce	¼ cup Jack Daniel's Tennessee Whiskey (optional)

In a medium-size pan, warm the barbecue sauce and add the whiskey. Stir until mixed and heated through. Keep warm on the stove or in a fondue pot.

FOR THE GRILLED CHICKEN

4 skinless, boneless breasts of chicken, halved	1 zip-top plastic bag, 1-gallon size
1 cup Italian salad dressing	

Marinate the chicken in the Italian salad dressing for 4 – 6 hours in a zip-top plastic bag. Preheat the grill to medium heat and grill for 7 minutes on each side, or until cooked through and the temperature reaches 165 degrees internally. Let rest, then cut into 1-inch cubes.

FOR THE PORK TENDERLOIN

2 1-pound pork tenderloins	2 tablespoons orange juice
½ cup soy sauce	1½ tablespoons fresh rosemary, finely chopped
½ cup dry sherry	1 tablespoon shallots, finely chopped
¼ cup honey	1 teaspoon fresh ginger, grated
¼ cup rice wine vinegar	1 teaspoon garlic, crushed
¼ cup vegetable oil	1 zip-top plastic bag, 1-gallon size

Combine the soy sauce, sherry, honey, vinegar, oil and orange juice in a medium bowl, whisking until well-blended. Stir in the rosemary, shallots, ginger and garlic. Set aside ½ cup for basting. Pour the mixture into a zip-top plastic bag, add the pork tenderloins and marinate overnight.

Bring pork to room temperature. Grill over medium-high heat or bake at 350 degrees for approximately 15 – 25 minutes. Baste often while cooking. Pork should reach 165 degrees internally. Let rest, then cut into 1-inch cubes.

Continued on following page

Barbecue with Chicken, Pork and Turkey Meatballs

FOR THE TURKEY MEATBALLS

1 pound ground turkey meat	2 tablespoons fresh flat-leaf parsley, chopped
¼ cup plain bread crumbs	2 teaspoons fresh thyme leaves, chopped
¼ cup grated parmesan cheese	1 egg, lightly beaten
½ cup onion, finely chopped	½ teaspoon salt
2 large cloves garlic, crushed	½ teaspoon ground black pepper

Preheat the oven to 400 degrees. Spray a baking sheet with cooking spray. In a large bowl, combine the turkey with the bread crumbs, parmesan cheese, onion, garlic, parsley, thyme, egg, salt and pepper. Form into 1-inch balls and place on a baking sheet. Bake for 10 – 15 minutes or until cooked through.

Serves 6 – 8

NOTE: YOU CAN SERVE THIS FONDUE WITH ANY PROTEIN YOU CHOOSE. OTHER OPTIONS INCLUDE SAUSAGE, CUBED TOFU, BEEF MEATBALLS, SKIRT STEAK AND CUBED TURKEY. TO SAVE TIME, YOU CAN BUY GRILLED CHICKEN BREASTS, COOKED PORK TENDERLOIN AND PRE-COOKED MEATBALLS AT YOUR LOCAL GROCERY STORE AND CUT THEM INTO CUBES TO USE IN THIS RECIPE.

Oil and Garlic with Poached Shrimp

FOR THE FONDUE

2 cups olive oil	1 tablespoon parsley, chopped
10 cloves garlic, chopped	Salt
6 anchovies	Pepper
½ teaspoon crushed red pepper flakes	

Pour the olive oil into a medium-size pan and heat over medium-low heat. When warm, add the garlic and turn the heat to low. Add the anchovies and stir as they dissolve and turn the oil brown. Add the pepper flakes and salt and pepper to taste. Just before pouring into your fondue pot or other heated serving vessel, add the parsley.

FOR THE SHRIMP

2 teaspoons salt	¼ cup fresh flat-leaf parsley, chopped
Juice of 2 lemons	¼ cup seafood seasoning
2 bay leaves	2 pounds jumbo shrimp, frozen,
¼ cup fresh thyme leaves	raw, shell-on

Defrost the shrimp according to directions on the package. Fill a large pot with a ½ gallon of water, add the salt, lemon juice, bay leaves, thyme, parsley and seafood seasoning. Bring to a boil over medium-high heat and simmer for 5 minutes to infuse the water with seasonings.

Reduce heat to medium-low and add the shrimp. Simmer, uncovered, for 5 minutes or until the shrimp are bright pink and the tails curl. Using a slotted spoon, remove the shrimp from the poaching liquid and refrigerate. When thoroughly chilled, peel off all of the shell from the shrimp so the whole thing can be dipped into the fondue.

Serves 6 – 8

NOTE: YOU CAN BUY THE PRE-COOKED FROZEN SHRIMP AND DEFROST THEM ACCORDING TO THE PACKAGE. TO ADD FLAVOR AFTER THEY ARE DEFROSTED, SQUEEZE A LEMON OVER THEM AND SPRINKLE WITH YOUR FAVORITE SEAFOOD SEASONING. EVEN THOUGH YOU OR YOUR GUESTS MIGHT NOT LIKE ANCHOVIES, YOU WILL LIKE THEM IN THIS RECIPE, AS THEY JUST ADD A SALTY, EARTHY FLAVOR TO THE OIL.

Bourbon with Bread Pudding and Strawberries

FOR THE FONDUE

1 cup unsalted butter, room temperature	1 pint heavy whipping cream
2 cups sugar	1 cup Woodford Reserve bourbon

In a heavy saucepan, heat the butter and sugar until melted and sugar is dissolved. Add the cream and bourbon, cook until silky smooth and light in color, about 15 minutes. Pour into fondue pot.

FOR THE BREAD PUDDING

7 tablespoons unsalted butter, melted	1 teaspoon freshly ground nutmeg
¼ cup unsalted butter, melted	1½ teaspoons ground cinnamon
16 cups lightly packed, day old (very dry) egg bread cubes, approximately 1 pound (2 loaves), crust removed	3 cups half & half
	¾ cup golden raisins, soaked in Woodford Reserve bourbon
3 eggs	¾ cup flaked coconut
1½ cups sugar	1 cup toasted pecans, coarsely chopped
2 tablespoons vanilla extract	

Preheat oven to 350 degrees. Pour 7 tablespoons butter into 13 x 9-inch baking pan; swirl it around to coat bottom and sides. Pour excess butter and additional ¼ cup butter into a small bowl; set aside. In a large bowl, beat eggs and sugar with an electric mixer until thickened and light lemon-colored, 3 – 4 minutes. Add vanilla, nutmeg, cinnamon, half & half, raisins, coconut, pecans and reserved butter, beat on low speed to combine. Place 1 layer of bread cubes in buttered baking dish. Pour half the liquid mixture over bread in baking dish, distributing nuts, coconut and raisins evenly. Continue to layer bread cubes and liquid mixture until both have been used. Press bread down into liquid often to make sure all cubes are covered. Set pan aside until bread has absorbed all of the liquid, 30 – 45 minutes. Bake in preheated oven until crusty and golden brown on top, 45 – 60 minutes. While pudding is baking, prepare the Bourbon Fondue. Cool bread pudding completely, then cut into, 1-inch squares for dipping.

Serves 18 – 20

NOTE: YOU CAN BUY BREAD PUDDING AT YOUR LOCAL GROCERY STORE AND CUT IT INTO 1-INCH SQUARES TO SERVE WITH THIS FONDUE. THIS FONDUE IS ALSO GOOD WITH STRAWBERRIES, POUND CAKE AND ANGEL FOOD CAKE.

Timeline

1 WEEK AHEAD
· Shop for non-perishable groceries

2 DAYS AHEAD
· Shop for last-minute groceries
· Put the frozen shrimp in the refrigerator to thaw for the Oil and Garlic Fondue with Shrimp.

1 DAY AHEAD
· Prepare the asparagus and red skin potatoes for the Brie and Wild Mushroom Fondue
· Poach the shrimp for the Oil and Garlic Fondue
· Make the bread pudding
· Marinate and grill the chicken for the Barbecue Fondue
· Make the marinade and marinate the pork tenderloin
· Make and cook the turkey meatballs
· Set out all of your skewers, used skewer vessels, napkins, small plates and glassware

MORNING OF THE PARTY
· Clean and chop mushrooms for the Brie and Wild Mushroom Fondue; refrigerate
· Remove the rind and cut the Brie for the Brie and Wild Mushroom Fondue; refrigerate
· Cook the pork tenderloin; refrigerate

2 HOURS AHEAD
· Cube the chicken and pork tenderloin
· Cut the bread pudding into bite-size pieces and plate

1 HOUR AHEAD
· Make the Brie and Wild Mushroom Fondue; keep warm
· Arrange and plate the asparagus and red skin potatoes for the Brie and Wild Mushroom Fondue
· Make the Oil and Garlic Fondue
· Make the Bourbon Fondue
· Plate the chicken, pork tenderloin and meatballs for the Barbecue Fondue

30 MINUTES BEFORE THE PARTY
· Cube baguettes and place on serving dish or in a basket
· Plate the shrimp for the Oil and Garlic Fondue
· Make the Barbecue Fondue

JUST BEFORE THE PARTY
· Put the fondues in each of their pots and keep warm as your guests arrive
· Check bar; put ice in bucket; set out sodas, waters, beer and wine

Shopping List

Asparagus, 2 bunches
Red skin potatoes, 2 pounds
Porcini mushrooms, dried,
    1 ounce
Shiitake mushrooms, fresh,
    8 ounces
Wheel of Brie, 1 pound
Jekel chardonnay
Baguette, 1
Anchovies, 1 jar
Flat-leaf parsley, 2 bunches
Lemons, 2
Jumbo shrimp, frozen, raw,
    shells-on, 2 pounds
Jack Daniel's Barbeque Sauce,
    1 28-ounce bottle
Jack Daniel's Tennessee
    Whiskey
Skinless, boneless breasts
    of chicken halves, 4
Italian salad dressing
2 1-pound pork tenderloins
Dry sherry
Orange juice
Rosemary, 1 bunch
Shallots, 4
Ginger, 1 knob
Garlic, 2 bulbs
Ground turkey meat, 1 pound
Plain bread crumbs
Parmesan cheese
Onion, 1
Thyme leaves, 2 bunches
Heavy whipping cream, 1 pint
Woodford Reserve bourbon
Egg bread, 1 pound (2 loaves)
Half & half, 1 quart
Golden raisins
Flaked coconut
Pecans

**ALSO BUY, IF NOT
IN YOUR PANTRY**
Soy sauce
Honey
Rice wine vinegar
Vegetable oil
Olive oil
Eggs
Unsalted butter
Sugar
Cornstarch
Chili flakes
Bay leaves
Seafood seasoning
Vanilla extract
Nutmeg
Cinnamon
Salt
Pepper
Wooden skewers
    of various lengths
Meat thermometer
Zip-top plastic bags,
    1-gallon size

The Big Game

The big game is on and that means a gathering of your favorite fans huddled around the TV supported by big food and snacks. We know hungry fans like to eat before, during and after the game. With this in mind, we have a solution that will keep everyone on the sidelines happy and satisfied with a winning lineup of food and beverages. Since this is a casual occasion, make it easy on yourself by using paper and plastic plates, napkins and utensils. Encourage your guests to show their team spirit by dressing in their favorite teams' colors. For the big game, offer the traditional foods and include a twist that will score with everyone. Our field of food will be a touchdown for light-to-heavy eaters, vegetarians and carnivores. We have you covered as your guests tackle the buffet table.

Start by setting up your field of food with the cooler station. Have a wide assortment of beverages, including a signature drink. Down the field is a crunch station. A good crunch station includes a crispy assortment of fresh vegetables and chips, complemented by several types of dips. Our Cool Everything Dip has a non-fat yogurt base which is big on flavor. To enhance a traditional dip, purchase your favorite brand of French Onion Dip and add a clove of crushed garlic and fresh chopped parsley to give it an extra kick.

Further down the field are halftime hits or entrées, including big wings and a build-your-own chili bar. The big wings are baked, which saves a lot of calories, but they are still crispy and delicious. The build-your-own chili bar starts with a vegetarian chili recipe and offers many accompaniments so your guests can build their own with the toppers they enjoy.

The end-zone keeps fans happy as they score easy-to-eat desserts. This is where you as a host can make it easy on yourself as well. Buy bite-sized items such as brownies, bars and cookies that can be set out early and last long after the game, because everyone loves desserts and not necessarily at the end of the night.

Big Game Cooler

The number one-ordered cocktail or drink in restaurants is the margarita. People love them and they are delicious. Margaritas also pair with a wide assortment of food and flavors. As the Big Game food table contains an assortment of flavors that are big and bold, the margarita is the perfect signature drink. It also is a drink that can be made easily in batches and will serve many. This is my award-winning recipe. You will find this drink so delicious you will want to use it every time you entertain. As an added twist, you can add a little food coloring to showcase your favorite teams' colors.

In a large bowl or container, mix the following:	2 12-ounce cans of frozen lemonade
2 750-ml bottles of 100% blue agave	1 12-ounce can of frozen limeade
tequila, such as el Jimador Blanco	1 gallon of water

This recipe makes about 34 servings, using 12-ounce cups filled with ice.

NOTE: MAKE SURE YOU HAVE PLENTY OF ALCOHOL-FREE BEVERAGE CHOICES AVAILABLE, INCLUDING BOTTLED WATER AND AN ASSORTMENT OF SOFT DRINKS

Cool Everything Dip

This non-fat dip works with everything from vegetables to wings to an assortment of chips, or even as a topper on chili in place of the standard sour cream.

1 cup non-fat plain yogurt (preferably Greek-style)	1 teaspoon garlic powder
1 tablespoon hot sauce	1 teaspoon dried ancho chili or chipotle chili powder (or a combination of the two)
1 teaspoon onion powder	

Combine yogurt, hot sauce, onion powder, garlic powder and chili powder together in a small bowl. This is best when made one day ahead so the flavors have time to blend.

Makes 1 cup

NOTE: YOU CAN ADD OR SUBTRACT THE HEAT TO SUIT YOUR TASTE. IF YOU LIKE IT HOT, ADD MORE HOT SAUCE AND CHILI POWDER.

Seasoned Potato Chips

1 large bag plain potato chips, your favorite variety and style	½ teaspoon ground black pepper
1 teaspoon garlic powder	½ teaspoon mustard powder
2 teaspoons Kosher salt	Pinch of chili powder

Preheat oven to 350 degrees. Spread potato chips out on a large baking sheet. In a small bowl, mix the garlic powder, Kosher salt, black pepper, mustard powder and chili powder. Heat the chips for 5 minutes or until the oil glistens. Remove from the oven and sprinkle with the seasoning mix. Toss in a bowl or platter and serve immediately.

Serves 8 – 10

Baked Wings

2 tablespoons paprika

3 tablespoons cayenne pepper

5 tablespoons fresh ground black pepper

6 tablespoons garlic powder

3 tablespoons onion powder

6 tablespoons salt

2½ tablespoons dried oregano

2½ tablespoons dried thyme

2 tablespoons Chinese five-spice powder

50 chicken wings, raw

In a small bowl, combine the paprika, cayenne pepper, black pepper, garlic powder, onion powder, salt, oregano, thyme and Chinese five-spice powder. Put 15 of the chicken wings in a large bowl and sprinkle liberally with ⅓ of the dry mixture. Toss until completely coated. Repeat the same process with 15 more wings, then the last 20 wings. After all the wings have been completely coated, place on a baking sheet and refrigerate for at least 2 hours.

Preheat oven to 350 degrees.

Spread chicken wings, in a single layer, on a baking sheet. Place in oven on middle rack. Bake for 1 hour until crispy, turning after 30 minutes. Serve with hot sauce and Cool Everything Dip.

Serves 8 – 10

Vegetarian Chili

1 tablespoon olive oil
6 cloves garlic, crushed
1 large onion, chopped
1 green pepper, chopped
1 red pepper, chopped
1 yellow pepper, chopped
1 10.75-ounce can puréed tomatoes

1 28-ounce can crushed tomatoes
1 4.5-ounce can diced green chilies
1 tablespoon ground cumin
1 tablespoon dried oregano
¼ teaspoon cayenne pepper
Juice of ½ lime
1 teaspoon ground black pepper

Heat the olive oil in a large pan and sauté the garlic, onion, green, red and yellow peppers until they just begin to soften. Add the puréed tomatoes, crushed tomatoes, green chilies, cumin, oregano, cayenne pepper, lime and pepper. Cover and simmer at least 1 hour and up to 2 hours.

Serves 6 – 8

SERVE WITH THE FOLLOWING ACCOMPANIMENTS
SO YOUR GUESTS CAN BUILD THEIR OWN

BLACK BEANS
KIDNEY BEANS
SPAGHETTI
HOT SAUCE
MEAT
CHEESE
ONIONS
OYSTER CRACKERS
FRITOS
COOL EVERYTHING DIP

Timeline

1 WEEK AHEAD
- Shop for non-perishable groceries
- Shop for Big Game-themed paper and plastic plates, napkins, utensils, tablecloths and other decorations

1 DAY AHEAD
- Shop for last-minute groceries
- Make the Signature Cocktail — Margarita; refrigerate
- Make the Cool Everything Dip; refrigerate
- Clean and chop the vegetables for the vegetable platter; store in zip-top plastic bags in refrigerator
- Add the garlic and parsley to the purchased French Onion Dip; refrigerate
- Make the Vegetarian Chili; refrigerate
- Cook the stew meat; refrigerate
- Cook the spaghetti; toss with a little olive oil to prevent sticking; refrigerate
- Put all the accompaniments for the chili in bowls and store in refrigerator, as needed

MORNING OF THE PARTY
- Make the spice mixture for the Seasoned Potato Chips
- Make the spice rub for the Baked Wings
- Toss the wings with the spice rub; refrigerate

2 HOURS AHEAD
- Heat the chili on stovetop or in slow cooker

1 HOUR AHEAD
- Bake the wings and plate
- Cut the purchased desserts into bite-sized pieces and arrange on a platter

JUST BEFORE THE PARTY
- Set out the Cool Everything Dip and vegetable platter
- Bake the Seasoned Potato Chips and toss with spice mix
- Set out the enhanced French Onion Dip
- Move the chili to your serving area
- Take out and arrange the chili accompaniments; slightly heat the meat and spaghetti
- Set out serving spoons / forks for all food items
- Set out the Signature Cocktail — Margarita — with plastic cups and ice
- Fill container with ice, waters and sodas
- Turn on all your TVs and make sure they are tuned into the Big Game

Shopping List

Non-fat plain yogurt
  (preferably Greek-style), 1 cup
French onion dip
Flat-leaf parsley, 1 bunch
Carrots, 1 bunch
Celery, 1 bunch
Broccoli, 3 crowns
Cherry tomatoes, 1 pint
Plain potato chips, 1 large bag
Chicken wings, 50, raw
Garlic, 1 bulb
Onion, 2 large
Green pepper, 1
Red pepper, 1
Yellow pepper, 1
Puréed tomatoes, 1 10.75-ounce can
Crushed tomatoes, 1 28-ounce can
Diced green chilies, 1 4.5-ounce can
Lime, 1
Black beans, 1 can
Kidney beans, 1 can
Spaghetti, 1 box
Stew meat, 1 pound
Cheddar cheese, 2 cups, shredded
Oyster crackers, 1 package
Fritos, 1 package
100% blue agave tequila, such as
  el Jimador Blanco, 2 750-ml bottles
Frozen lemonade, 2 12-ounce cans
Frozen limeade, 1 12-ounce can
Brownies
Bars
Cookies

ALSO BUY, IF NOT IN YOUR PANTRY

Hot sauce
Onion powder
Garlic powder
Ancho chili and/or
  chipotle chili powder
Kosher salt
Black pepper
Mustard powder
Paprika
Cayenne pepper
Dried oregano
Dried thyme
Chinese five-spice powder
Ground cumin
Dried oregano
Olive oil

Valentine's Day

February 14th is Valentine's Day, an occasion to enjoy a special meal for two (or more) at home. The secret here is you don't have to wait until February 14th. This dinner can be enjoyed any day of the year.

When thinking of romance or a romantic dinner, Italy comes to mind. Maybe it's the image of Walt Disney's *Lady and the Tramp* and the famous spaghetti scene, or memories of candlelight dinners with soft Italian music playing in the background. You can create your own romantic setting with a bistro table, candles, wine, delicious pasta and a sweet ending. Now that's amore!

MENU

CUPID'S COCKTAIL

PESTO PEPPERS

THIS CAESAR SALAD RULES, WITH GARLIC AND HERB CROUTONS AND PARMESAN TUILES

PASTA ANGELO

GARLIC TOAST

BLACK RASPBERRY WHIPPED CREAM WITH BERRIES

WINE SUGGESTIONS

PINOT GRIGIO OR SAUVIGNON BLANC WITH THE CAESAR SALAD

CHIANTI OR MERLOT WITH THE PASTA ANGELO

PINK CHAMPAGNE WITH WHIPPED CREAM AND BERRIES

Cupid's Cocktail

3 ounces vodka

6 ounces cranberry juice

1 ounce Chambord liqueur

Gummy candy hearts for garnish

In a shaker with ice, combine the vodka, cranberry juice and Chambord. Shake until cold and strain into martini glasses. Garnish with spears of gummy candy hearts.

Serves 2

Pesto Peppers

1 red pepper, seeded, cut into ½-inch strips
1 yellow pepper, seeded, cut into
   ½-inch strips
1 orange bell pepper, seeded, cut into
   ½-inch strips
4 anchovies, chopped
2 tablespoons fresh oregano, finely chopped
3 cloves garlic, finely chopped

2 tablespoons capers, drained and chopped
¼ cup extra virgin olive oil
¼ teaspoon black pepper

In a small bowl, combine the anchovies, oregano, garlic, capers, olive oil and black pepper. Refrigerate for at least 2 hours or overnight.

Preheat oven to 400 degrees.

Place peppers on baking sheet and bake for 15 minutes until just tender. Cool to room temperature. Spread a small amount of the pesto on each of the peppers. Serve at room temperature.

Serves 4 – 6

Garlic and Herb Croutons

These croutons will add a wonderful aroma to your home. The recipe makes a few extra as it is hard to resist sneaking one or two from the pan as they cook.

4 cups bread (preferably baguette), cut into 1-inch cubes	½ teaspoon dried oregano
	½ teaspoon dried basil
2 tablespoons butter	½ teaspoon dried parsley
2 tablespoons olive oil	½ teaspoon Kosher salt
4 cloves garlic, crushed	½ teaspoon ground black pepper

In a large sauté pan, melt the butter with the olive oil over medium heat. Once melted, reduce the heat to low, add the garlic and sauté until combined. Add the bread cubes and toss to coat evenly. Sprinkle the salt and pepper over the cubes and continue to cook on low heat for 10 minutes, stirring occasionally. Add the oregano, basil and parsley and cook for an additional 10 minutes, stirring occasionally. The cubes will begin to dry and brown slightly. Store at room temperature until ready to serve.

Serves 4 – 6

NOTE: THE COMBINATION OF DRIED OREGANO, BASIL AND PARSLEY IS A WONDERFUL MIX WHICH CAN BE SPRINKLED ON PASTAS, VEGETABLES, MASHED POTATOES AND MANY OTHER DISHES. STORE THIS IN A JAR IN YOUR PANTRY. SIMPLY COMBINE EQUAL PARTS OF THE THREE HERBS.

Parmesan Tuiles

1 cup parmesan cheese, freshly grated	Rolling pin
Silpat or parchment paper	

Preheat oven to 350 degrees.

Place the Silpat or parchment paper on a baking sheet. Using ¼ cup of the cheese, form into a 3-inch round. Repeat with the remaining cheese to make a total of 4 rounds spaced 1 inch apart. Bake for 6 – 8 minutes or until bubbling and golden. Let cool for 2 minutes, then carefully remove with a spatula and form around a rolling pin. Let cool completely.

Serves 4

NOTE: THE BAKED CHEESE CAN ALSO BE FORMED AROUND SMALL BOWLS TO MAKE CUPS, OR COOLED FLAT AND CUT INTO STRIPS. A SILPAT IS A NON-STICK BAKING MAT MADE OF FIBERGLASS AND SILICONE.

This Caesar Salad Rules

3 cloves garlic, crushed
1 teaspoon anchovy paste
4 tablespoons olive oil
2 teaspoons stone-ground mustard
Juice of ½ lime
1 tablespoon red wine vinegar

½ teaspoon Worcestershire sauce
Dash of Tabasco
¼ cup freshly grated parmesan cheese
½ teaspoon ground black pepper
2 hearts of romaine, washed and
    torn into bite-size pieces

In a large salad bowl, preferably wood, add the garlic and anchovy paste. Mash together with a fork. Add the olive oil, mustard, lime juice, red wine vinegar, Worcestershire sauce and Tabasco. Mix vigorously. Add the parmesan cheese and black pepper. Mix until incorporated. Toss with romaine lettuce and plate immediately. Garnish with Garlic and Herb Croutons and Parmesan Tuiles.

Serves 4 – 6

Pasta Angelo

This is a delicious, flavorful and easy-to-make pasta. What sets it apart is the added flavor of the bacon and a touch of cream.

2 slices bacon	2 tablespoons heavy cream
1 shallot, chopped	2 teaspoons dried basil
4 cloves garlic, crushed	2 teaspoons dried oregano
1 14.5-ounce can diced or crushed tomatoes	2 teaspoons fresh flat-leaf parsley, chopped
1 15-ounce can tomato sauce	¼ cup freshly grated parmesan cheese
1 teaspoon sugar	1 box angel hair pasta
¼ teaspoon black pepper	Olive oil
Pinch of salt	

Cook pasta until it is still slightly firm or *al dente*. This might be less time than what is recommended on the package. Drizzle pasta with a little olive oil to prevent sticking. Set aside.

In a large sauté pan, cook bacon over medium heat to render the fat. Do not burn. Discard the bacon and add the shallots and garlic to the pan. Sauté until soft, about 4 minutes. Add the crushed tomatoes, tomato sauce, sugar, pepper, salt and simmer for 5 minutes. Add the cream, basil and oregano and simmer for an additional 2 minutes. Add desired amount of pasta to the pan and toss with the sauce to coat and cook until just heated through. Garnish with parmesan cheese and parsley.

Serves 4 – 6

Garlic Toast

15 slices of bread (preferably baguette), approximately ½-inch thick	4 tablespoons butter, melted
3 cloves garlic	Kosher salt

Preheat oven to 400 degrees.

Place bread on baking sheet in a single layer. Bake for 5 minutes. While still hot, rub the bread with the raw garlic cloves. They will melt as you rub over the surface. Brush with melted butter and sprinkle with Kosher salt. Serve warm.

Serves 4 – 6

Black Raspberry Whipped Cream with Berries

1 pint heavy whipping cream	3 tablespoons Chambord liqueur
¼ cup powdered sugar	3 cups fresh strawberries

In a mixer with a wire whisk attachment, combine the cream, powdered sugar and Chambord. Whip on low for 30 seconds to incorporate, then on high for 3 – 4 minutes until stiff peaks form. Be careful not to over-whip. Serve in a martini glass surrounded by strawberries.

Serves 4 – 6

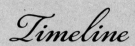

Timeline

1 WEEK AHEAD
- Shop for non-perishable groceries
- Shop for Valentine's Day cards, candy and decorations

1 DAY AHEAD
- Shop for last-minute groceries
- Set the table
- Make the pesto for the Pesto Peppers

MORNING OF THE PARTY
- Clean and slice the peppers for the Pesto Peppers; refrigerate until baking
- Wash and tear the romaine lettuce for This Caesar Salad Rules; refrigerate in a zip-top plastic bag with paper towel to absorb the moisture.
- Make the Garlic and Herb Croutons; store at room temperature
- Make the Parmesan Tuiles; store at room temperature
- Clean the strawberries
- Make the whipped cream for the Black Raspberry Whipped Cream and Berries

2 HOURS AHEAD
- Set out the ingredients in pre-measured bowls for This Caesar Salad Rules

1 HOUR AHEAD
- Bake the peppers for the Pesto Peppers
- Cook the angel hair pasta for the Pasta Angelo

JUST BEFORE THE PARTY
- Set out ingredients for the Cupid's Cocktail and shake when ready
- Assemble and plate the Pesto Peppers
- Make the Pasta Angelo; keep warm in the pan
- Make the Garlic Toast
- Turn on romantic music
- Light candles

DURING THE PARTY
- Make the Caesar dressing; assemble and serve This Caesar Salad Rules

WHEN READY FOR DESSERT
- Plate the Black Raspberry Whipped Cream and Berries

Shopping List

Red pepper, 1
Yellow pepper, 1
Orange bell pepper, 1
Anchovies, 1 jar
Oregano, 1 bunch
Capers, 1 jar
Anchovy paste, 1 tube
Stone-ground mustard
Lime, 1
Hearts of romaine, 2
Baguette, 1
Garlic, 2 bulbs
Parmesan cheese
Bacon, 2 slices
Shallot, 1
Diced or crushed tomatoes,
   1 14.5-ounce can
Tomato sauce, 1 15-ounce can
Flat-leaf parsley, 1 bunch
Angel hair pasta, 1 box
Heavy cream, 1 quart
Fresh strawberries
Vodka
Korbel Brut Rosé champagne
Cranberry juice
Chambord liqueur
Gummy candy hearts for garnish

ALSO BUY, IF NOT IN YOUR PANTRY

Butter
Olive oil
Dried oregano
Dried basil
Dried parsley
Kosher salt
Ground black pepper
Sugar
Red wine vinegar
Worcestershire sauce
Tabasco
Powdered sugar

CÉAD MÍLE
FÁILTE

St. Patrick's Day

St. Patrick's Day

St. Patrick's Day, March 17th, is when everyone becomes Irish for the day, making this a fun entertaining occasion. Depending on when St. Patrick's Day falls, you can entertain either on the day, the weekend before or the weekend after. Many people think of St. Patrick's not as one day but as a season and continue the celebration all month long as he was considered the most commonly recognized of the patron saints of Ireland.

You can start your St. Patrick's Day celebration at home with a festive breakfast of green eggs and ham. Yes, you can! For a fun-themed party, serve traditional corned beef, cabbage, green mashed potatoes (made with fresh pea purée) and soda bread. Another hearty option is a warm bowl of Irish Stout Beef Stew. For beverages, consider Irish Black and Tans or festive green drinks like my Sparkling Shamrock. For dessert, it's Irish Coffee!

Don't forget your Irish toast. Here are a few of my favorites:

*May you be in
Heaven a half hour before the
Devil knows you're dead!*

*May your blessings outnumber
the shamrocks that grow,
and may trouble avoid you
wherever you go.*

*There are many good reasons for drinking,
one has just entered my head.
If a man doesn't drink when he's living,
how in the hell can he drink when he's dead?*

*May the best day of your past
be the worst day of your future.*

*My friends are the best friends
loyal, willing and able.
Now let's get to drinking!
All glasses off the table!*

Sláinte!

St. Patrick's Day Drinks

IRISH COFFEE

In a mug, add:
1½ ounces Irish whiskey
3 ounces black coffee

Top with whipped cream and a splash of green Crème de Menthe.
Serves 1

LEPRECHAUN'S BELT

In a shaker with ice, add:
3 ounces Finlandia vodka
2 ounces apple liqueur

Shake and strain into cocktail glasses. Garnish with green apple slices.
Serves 2

SPARKLING SHAMROCK

In a white wine glass, add:
3 ounces Korbel champagne
1 ounce melon liqueur
Serves 1

GREEN AGAVE

In a shaker with ice, add:
3 ounces 100% blue agave tequila, such as Herradura Silver
1½ ounces melon liqueur
2 ounces fresh lime juice
1 ounce agave nectar

Shake and pour into rocks glasses. Garnish with lime wedges.
Serves 2

Green Eggs and Ham and Sparkling Shamrock

This is a fun and easy way to turn your breakfast into a St. Patrick's Day treat. Simply add several drops of green food coloring (until desired color) to your beaten eggs for scrambled eggs. Cook according to your liking and serve with a slice of ham that has been browned in the skillet and your favorite breakfast potatoes.

Roasted Potatoes with Smoked Salmon

½ pound small red potatoes
2 tablespoons olive oil
½ teaspoon salt

8 ounces smoked salmon, cut into
   bite-size pieces
Fresh dill sprigs

Preheat oven to 450 degrees.

Cut the ends off the potatoes then continue cutting crosswise into ¼-inch slices. Repeat with the remaining potatoes. Place the potato slices in a bowl and toss with olive oil and salt until well-coated. Place the slices in a single layer on a baking sheet and bake for 10 minutes. Flip, and continue cooking for 10 minutes until golden. Remove from the oven and let cool. Top with smoked salmon pieces and fresh dill sprigs.

Serves 6 – 8

Oven-Roasted Corned Beef

1 3-pound corned beef brisket	2 tablespoons pickling spice

Preheat oven to 300 degrees.

Sprinkle the brisket, fat-side-up, with pickling spice. Wrap the brisket in foil and place in a shallow baking dish, fat-side-up. Bake for 3 hours, or 1 hour per pound. Let rest for 15 minutes, then slice across the grain and serve.

Serves 6 – 8

Mashed Potatoes with Pea Purée

The pea purée adds a festive color and wonderful texture to everyday mashed potatoes.

1 pound Yukon Gold potatoes, peeled and cut into 1-inch cubes	¼ cup milk, possibly a little more
1 pound Idaho potatoes, peeled and cut into 1-inch cubes	3 tablespoons butter
1 tablespoon salt	1 16-ounce bag frozen peas, thawed
	Salt
	Black pepper

Boil potatoes in a large saucepan of boiling salted water until tender, about 12 minutes. Drain well. Return potatoes to the same pan. Add milk and butter. Mash until smooth, adding additional milk for desired consistency. In a blender or food processor, purée the peas until smooth. Mix the purée into the mashed potatoes. Season to taste with salt and pepper.

Serves 6 – 8

NOTE: FOR PLAIN MASHED POTATOES, SIMPLY LEAVE OUT THE PEA PURÉE.

Steamed Cabbage

1 large head of cabbage	Salt
Butter	Pepper

Cut the cabbage in half and then each half into 4 wedges to make a total of 8 wedges. In a large pot with a steamer basket, bring 1 inch of water to a boil. Place the cabbage in the pot. Cover and steam for 10 minutes until fork-tender. Do not overcook. Serve with butter, salt and pepper.

Serves 6 – 8

Irish Stout Beef Stew

⅓ cup olive oil
1½ pounds stew meat cut into 1-inch cubes
8 cloves garlic, crushed
3 14-ounce cans (6 cups) low sodium
  beef broth
1 cup Irish stout beer
1 cup cabernet sauvignon wine
2 tablespoons tomato paste
1 teaspoon sugar
1 tablespoon dried thyme

1 tablespoon Worcestershire sauce
2 bay leaves
3 large carrots, peeled and
  cut into ½-inch slices
3 pounds Idaho potatoes, peeled and
  cut into 1-inch cubes
1 12-ounce package frozen pearl onions
Salt
Pepper

In a large pan, heat the oil over medium-high heat. Add the meat and brown on each side, approximately 5 minutes. You may need to do this in batches so as not to overcrowd the pan. With all the meat in the pan, add the garlic and sauté, then add the beef broth, beer and wine, scraping the bottom of the pan to release the brown bits. Add the tomato paste, sugar, thyme, Worcestershire sauce and bay leaves. Bring to a boil, then reduce heat to low. Cover and simmer for 60 minutes. Add the carrots, potatoes and pearl onions, and simmer uncovered for an additional 30 minutes or until the vegetables are tender. Remove the bay leaves and serve with Irish Soda Bread. Can be made 2 days ahead of time.

Serves 6 – 8

NOTE: ANOTHER SERVING IDEA IS TO HOLLOW OUT A BREAD BOULE, FILL WITH BEEF STEW, TOP WITH MASHED POTATOES AND CHEDDAR CHEESE. HEAT UNDER THE BROILER TO MELT THE CHEESE.

Irish Soda Bread

2 cups flour
2 teaspoons baking powder
1 teaspoon baking soda
½ teaspoon salt
1 tablespoon sugar
2 tablespoons unsalted butter, cold,
    cut into small pieces

2 tablespoons solid vegetable shortening,
    cold, cut into small pieces
1 egg, lightly beaten
1 cup buttermilk
1 cup raisins
1 tablespoon caraway seeds, toasted
1 tablespoon butter, melted
1 tablespoon turbinado or raw sugar

Preheat oven to 375 degrees.

In a large bowl, combine the flour, baking powder, baking soda, salt and sugar. Add the butter and shortening to the flour mixture, using your hands to work it in. It should look and feel like coarse meal. Add the egg and buttermilk slowly, to incorporate. Add the raisins and caraway seeds, then mix thoroughly. Transfer the dough to a floured surface and knead for a couple minutes until it forms a ball. Additional flour may be needed if the dough is too sticky. Place the dough into a lightly greased loaf pan. Score the top in a criss-cross pattern with a sharp knife. Brush the top with melted butter and sprinkle with the turbinado or raw sugar. Bake for 40 minutes or until golden brown. When a toothpick is inserted, it should come out clean.

Serves 6 – 8

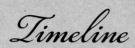

Timeline

1 WEEK AHEAD
- Shop for non-perishable groceries
- Shop for St. Patrick's Day decorations

2 DAYS AHEAD
- Shop for last-minute groceries
- Set your table with platters, serving pieces and decorations
- Make the Irish Stout Beef Stew

1 DAY AHEAD
- Set up the bar
- Make bar garnishes

MORNING OF THE PARTY
- Make the Irish Soda Bread; store at room temperature

2 HOURS AHEAD
- Brew coffee and keep warm in a thermos
- Make the potato chips for the base of the Roasted Potatoes with Smoked Salmon
- Roast the Corned Beef; it should be ready as you are ending cocktail hour.

1 HOUR AHEAD
- Heat the Irish Stout Beef Stew on the stove and keep warm until serving
- Make the Mashed Potatoes; keep warm

JUST BEFORE THE PARTY
- Plate the Roasted Potatoes with Smoked Salmon
- Slice and plate the Irish Soda Bread
- Set out all other food items
- Check bar; put ice in bucket; set out garnishes
- During cocktail hour and just before serving, steam the Cabbage
- After letting the Corned Beef rest, slice and serve warm

Shopping List

Stew meat, 1½ pounds
Garlic, 1 bulb
Beef broth, low sodium,
  3 14-ounce cans (6 cups)
Irish stout beer, 1 can
Cabernet Sauvignon wine, 1 bottle
Carrots, 3 large
Idaho potatoes, 4 pounds
Frozen pearl onions, 1 12-ounce bag
Bread boule (optional)
Cheddar cheese (optional)
Corned beef brisket, 3 pounds
Pickling spice
Cabbage, 1 large head
Yukon Gold potatoes, 1 pound
Small red potatoes, ½ pound
Smoked salmon, 8 ounces
Fresh dill, 1 bunch
Buttermilk
Caraway seeds
Turbinado or raw sugar
Irish whiskey
Crème de Menthe
Finlandia vodka
Apple liqueur
Green apples
Korbel champagne
Melon liqueur
100% blue agave tequila,
  such as Herradura Silver
Limes, 2
Agave nectar

ALSO BUY, IF NOT
IN YOUR PANTRY
Olive oil
Tomato paste
Sugar
Dried thyme
Worcestershire sauce
Bay leaves
Kosher salt
Black pepper
Unsalted butter
Milk
Flour
Baking powder
Baking soda
Solid vegetable shortening
Eggs
Raisins
Coffee
Whipped Cream

Game Night

Rain, sleet, snow, cold or whenever…have an entertaining party inside with game night at home. Many classic board games have been forgotten, given the electronic era of games. Put the plug-in games away and grab one or two of the classics and pair them with easy and fun to make food and beverages.

For game night, nothing is easier than having a variety of hot dogs, beers, French fries and a complete ice cream sundae bar. You can even make a game out of designing your own "dog" and sundae. For an added twist, bring in local flavors to personalize your hot dog. We live in Louisville, Kentucky, and serve hot dogs similar to the locally famous Hot Brown* and another one using Henry Bain Sauce.** You can design a German rendition with bratwurst, spicy mustard and red cabbage. Go meat-free with tofu dogs, avocado, sprouts and yellow peppers. There are no limits in the hot dog design game. For the beer selections, we have Root Beer and Beer Margaritas. Dessert is a serve yourself, build-your-own sundae bar with a wide assortment of toppings. As with any game, big decisions have to be made on the board, on the plate and in the bowl.

---

*   A famous sandwich created in the 1920s at the Brown Hotel in Louisville, Kentucky consisting of bread, turkey, bacon, tomato and Mornay sauce.

** A sauce for meat created by Henry Bain (1863-1928), a legendary waiter at the Pendennis Club in Louisville, Kentucky.

Beer Margaritas

24 ounces cold beer, light in style such as a pilsner

½ cup frozen limeade, thawed

½ cup 100% blue agave tequila such as El Jimador Blanco

1 lime, sliced (reserve a few slices to rim the glasses)

In a pitcher, add all ingredients and pour into prepared rocks glasses with ice.

Serves 4

NOTE: SINCE NOT EVERYONE LIKES SALT ON A GLASS, RIM ONLY ⅓ OF THE GLASS WITH SALT TO PLEASE ALL OF YOUR GUESTS. MAKE A SIGNATURE SALT BY COMBINING KOSHER SALT WITH LEMON AND LIME ZEST. USE A LIME WEDGE TO WET THE EDGE OF THE GLASS, THEN DIP INTO A PLATE OF YOUR SALT MIXTURE. THE GLASSES CAN BE PREPARED EARLIER IN THE DAY.

GAME NIGHT

Baked French Fries

2 pounds russet potatoes, peeled and cut lengthwise into ½-inch-thick sticks 2 tablespoons olive oil	Kosher salt Fresh ground black pepper

Put a rimmed baking sheet on the middle rack of your oven and preheat the oven to 450 degrees.

Rinse the potatoes in a large pot of cold water, being careful not to break the sticks. Dry in a kitchen towel, then carefully toss in a large bowl with the olive oil. Remove the hot baking sheet from the oven and arrange the potatoes in a single layer. Roast the potatoes for 35 - 45 minutes, turning every 10 minutes until evenly browned. Sprinkle with salt and pepper, and serve immediately.

Serves 4 – 6

NOTE: INDIVIDUAL SERVINGS CAN BE MADE BY PUTTING PARCHMENT PAPER OR A COCKTAIL NAPKIN IN SMALL CUPS, AND FILLING WITH THE FRIES.

Marinated Cucumbers

⅓ cup sugar	1 teaspoon fresh ground black pepper
⅓ cup rice wine vinegar	2 English cucumbers, thinly sliced
1 teaspoon Kosher salt	1 tablespoon fresh snipped dill

In a large bowl, combine the sugar, vinegar, salt and pepper. Add the cucumbers and toss to coat. Cover and refrigerate for 2 hours. Just before serving, toss with the dill. Serve cold or at room temperature.

Serves 4 – 6

Spicy Horseradish Mustard

½ cup whole grain mustard	⅛ cup prepared horseradish
¼ cup Dijon mustard	1 tablespoon honey

In a small bowl, combine the whole grain mustard, Dijon mustard, horseradish and honey. Pour into a jar with a tight-fitting lid and store in the refrigerator. Can be made 1 week ahead.

Makes 1 cup

NOTE: IN ADDITION TO HOTDOGS, THIS MUSTARD IS GREAT ON HAMBURGERS, SANDWICHES AND AS A DIP FOR PRETZELS.

Easy Mornay Sauce

2 cups heavy whipping cream	Pinch of salt
1½ cups Monterey Jack cheese, shredded	Pinch of white pepper
½ cup white wine	2 teaspoons cornstarch
½ teaspoon smoked paprika	2 teaspoons white wine
Pinch of garlic powder	

In a small bowl, combine the cornstarch and the 2 teaspoons of white wine until dissolved into a slurry.

In a small sauce pan over medium heat, bring the cream to a gentle simmer. Whisk in the cheese and once it is incorporated add the ½ cup white wine, smoked paprika, garlic powder, salt and pepper while continuing to whisk. Let simmer for 5 minutes then add the cornstarch/white wine slurry while whisking well for 2 minutes. This will thicken the sauce. If you want to change the consistency, add more wine to thin it out or more slurry to thicken it.

Serve this on your Hot Brown Dog with bacon and sliced tomatoes.

Henry Bain Sauce

1 12-ounce bottle chili sauce
1 20-ounce bottle catsup
1 10-ounce bottle steak sauce

1 10-ounce bottle Worcestershire sauce
2 9-ounce bottles chutney

In a food processor, combine the chili sauce, catsup, steak sauce, Worcestershire sauce and chutney. Process until smooth.

The sauce will keep indefinitely refrigerated. It has many uses such as on chicken, beef and with French-fried potatoes.

Makes about 5 cups

Hot Dog Varieties

Here is a collection of our favorite dogs. Have fun creating your own combinations with ingredients indigenous to your area, favorite part of the country or world.

HOT BROWN
Turkey hot dog with bacon, sliced tomatoes and Easy Mornay Sauce

LOUISVILLE
Bison hot dog with Henry Bain Sauce

GREEK
Beef hot dog with spinach, red onion, black olives, Greek yogurt and feta cheese

CALIFORNIA
Tofu hot dog with avocado, sprouts and diced yellow peppers

SPRING ROLL
Pork hot dog with shredded carrots, cilantro, shrimp and Sriracha hot sauce

FRENCH
Beef hot dog with caramelized onions and Brie cheese

REUBEN
Beef hot dog with sauerkraut, Swiss cheese and Russian dressing

GERMAN
Bratwurst with Spicy Horseradish Mustard and red cabbage

SOUTH OF THE BORDER
Beef hot dog with Monterey Jack cheese, pico de gallo and jalapeños

Sundae Bar

This is a fun treat! Buy a gallon of your favorite ice cream, scoop out individual scoops and place in a large footed bowl. After all the ice cream is scooped into the footed bowl, put it in the freezer so when it is time to serve, your guests can easily put a scoop of ice cream in their dish and begin building their own personalized sundae.

The sky's the limit in terms of toppings, but here are a few of our favorites:

FUDGE SAUCE	SPRINKLES
CARAMEL SAUCE	M&M's
TOASTED PECANS	CRUSHED BUTTERFINGER BARS
FRESH SLICED STRAWBERRIES	CRUSHED HEATH BARS
FRESH RASPBERRIES	CHOCOLATE CHIPS
FRESH BLUEBERRIES	CRUSHED PRETZELS
CHERRIES	WHIPPED CREAM

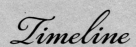

Timeline

1 WEEK AHEAD
- Shop for non-perishable groceries
- Check your stock of games or buy new ones
- Make a list of the types of hot dogs you plan to serve and all of the toppings

2 DAYS AHEAD
- Prepare your table with games, platters and serving pieces
- Make the Spicy Horseradish Mustard
- Make the Henry Bain Sauce for the Louisville Dog

1 DAY AHEAD
- Shop for last-minute groceries
- Chill mugs for the Root Beer

MORNING OF THE PARTY
- Scoop and freeze the ice cream and put the toppings into individual bowls for the Sundae Bar
- Prepare the toppings for your Hot Dogs
- Rim the glasses for the Beer Margaritas

2 HOURS AHEAD
- Make the Marinated Cucumbers

JUST BEFORE THE PARTY
- Set up the games
- Set out the Root Beer
- Make the Beer Margaritas
- Make the Easy Mornay Sauce for the Hot Brown Dog

WHILE YOUR GUESTS ARE PLAYING THEIR FIRST GAME
- Prepare and set out the Hot Dogs
- Make and plate the Baked French Fries
- Plate the Marinated Cucumbers

Join your guests for the next round of games. Afterward, set out the bowls and toppings for your Sundae Bar and, at the last-minute, the ice cream.

Shopping List

Your favorite brand and
   type of hot dogs
Hot dog toppings
Ice cream
Sundae toppings
Rice wine vinegar
English cucumbers, 2
Fresh dill, 1 bunch
Russet potatoes, 2 pounds
Whole grain mustard
Dijon mustard
Prepared horseradish, 1 bottle
Chili sauce, 12-ounce bottle
Catsup, 20-ounce bottle
Steak sauce, 10-ounce bottle
Worcestershire sauce,
   10-ounce bottle
Chutney, 2 9-ounce bottles
Heavy whipping cream, 1 pint
Shredded Monterey Jack cheese,
   1 bag
White wine
Beer, 24 ounces, light in style
   such as a pilsner
Frozen limeade, 1 can
100% blue agave tequila
   such as El Jimador Blanco
Lime, 1
Lemon, 1
Root Beer

ALSO BUY, IF NOT
IN YOUR PANTRY
Sugar
Kosher salt
Black pepper
Smoked paprika
Garlic powder
White pepper
Cornstarch
Olive oil
Honey

Derby Party

The first Saturday in May hosts "The Most Exciting Two Minutes in Sports." It is the Kentucky Derby! The Kentucky Derby is viewed by millions of people around the world and now is the focus of Derby-themed parties far beyond Louisville and Kentucky. It is also the perfect time to host a party, as it is always on a Saturday and the kickoff to party season. There has been a lull since the holidays and spring is blooming so in my book, that means it's party time. Break out the roses, hats, juleps and more for an exciting Derby Party at home.

TIPS ON HOSTING A DERBY PARTY

- The type of invitation you use will set the tone of the party – casual, formal and/or costume. Costume ideas include: dress in your favorite jockey's silks, creative hats required, or dress in the color of your Derby horse's saddle cloth.
- Saddle cloth colors correspond to the same number at almost all Thoroughbred racetracks. They help chart callers and fans identify the horses as they race.

1 RED	8 PINK	15 KHAKI
2 WHITE	9 TURQUOISE	16 COPEN BLUE
3 BLUE	10 PURPLE	17 NAVY
4 YELLOW	11 GRAY	18 FOREST GREEN
5 GREEN	12 LIME	19 MOONSTONE
6 BLACK	13 BROWN	20 FUCHSIA
7 ORANGE	14 MAROON	

- There are a variety of parties you can host: An early Derby breakfast / late morning brunch if you are planning to go to the track, or an afternoon cocktail party and dinner if you plan to watch the races at home.
- If you plan to watch the races at home, invite guests over 2 hours before the actual Derby Race so you can enjoy a few cocktails and appetizers as the anticipation for the race builds.
- Greet each guest with a mint julep, using the Mint Juleps for Many recipe.
- Get racing forms and programs from friends who have been to the track for decorating your table, or order them online.
- Red roses in julep cups and scattered red rose petals are traditional decorations.
- Garnish your table and food items with mint and red rose petals.
- Download or print the racing schedule so you know who is in the Derby race. Make multiple copies to have enough for all of your guests.
- For larger parties, and to be more economical, make punches or pitcher drinks of the Oaks Lily and Mint Julep. Not only does this cut down on cost, but also makes it easier on the host as guests serve themselves.
- Another idea to make it easier on the host is to have each guest bring an appetizer or dessert and give prizes for the best named and themed dishes, such as: Dead Heat "Spicy Nuts," Triple Crown "Crab Dip," Daily Double "Nut Brownies," Turf Track "Treats."
- As hats are a Derby tradition, you can host an outrageous hat contest and offer prizes for the best hat at your party.
- Set up a game of horseshoes in the backyard for entertainment leading up to the big race.

WAYS TO BET AT HOME PARTIES
- Set a price for each ticket. Have your guests who want to participate each buy a slip of paper (ticket) and have them write their name and the name of the horse they want to win the race. Guests may buy as many tickets as they want. As soon as the results are official, count the number of winning tickets and divide that number into the total money bet to determine the payoff per winning ticket.
- Set a price for each chance at choosing the winning horse. Write the names of each horse on a slip of paper and put them in a hat. Have each person who has bought a chance draw one of the slips of paper. Once the results are official, the person with the winning horse wins all the money.

Mint Juleps for Many

4 ounces Woodford Reserve bourbon	Crushed ice
2 ounces Mint Simple Syrup	Mint sprigs

Combine all ingredients in tall glasses. Add sipping straws and garnish with mint sprigs.

Serves 2

TO MAKE THE MINT SIMPLE SYRUP

1 part water
1 part sugar
1 part loosely-packed fresh mint leaves

In a saucepan, combine the water and sugar. Bring to a boil, stirring to dissolve the sugar. When the water is clear and the sugar is dissolved, remove from the heat and stir in the mint leaves. Let steep for 20 minutes. Strain into a glass container and store in the refrigerator for up to 1 week.

TO MAKE BY THE PITCHER

16 ounces Woodford Reserve bourbon
8 ounces Mint Simple Syrup

Mix ingredients. Pour into tall glasses filled with crushed ice. Garnish with mint sprigs and sipping straws.

Serves 8

NOTE: YOU CAN ADJUST THE SWEETNESS OF THE DRINK BY ADDING MORE OR LESS OF THE MINT SIMPLE SYRUP. THE MINT SIMPLE SYRUP IS ALSO A GREAT ADDITION TO ICED TEA.

Oaks Lily

2 ounces Finlandia vodka	Splash of triple sec
2 ounce sweet and sour mix	6 blackberries
6 ounces cranberry juice	

Add all ingredients to a shaker with ice. Shake until cold, strain into tall glasses filled with crushed ice. Garnish with blackberries on skewers. Add sipping straws and enjoy.

Serves 2

TO MAKE BY THE PITCHER

8 ounces Finlandia vodka

8 ounces sweet and sour mix

24 ounces cranberry juice

½ ounce triple sec

24 blackberries

> TIP: THIS CAN BE MADE AHEAD OF TIME AND STORED IN THE REFRIGERATOR UNTIL SERVING TIME.

Combine all ingredients. Pour into tall glasses filled with crushed ice. Garnish with blackberries on skewers. Add sipping straws and enjoy.

Serves 8

Oaks Lily Punch

16 ounces Finlandia vodka	24 ounces (2 12-ounce cans)
8 ounces sweet and sour mix	lemon-lime soda or ginger ale
24 ounces cranberry juice	1 pint blackberries
1 ounce triple sec	

Pour all ingredients into a punch bowl. Garnish with frozen blackberries and/or frozen ice block to keep chilled.

Serves: 15 – 20

> NOTE: THIS DRINK DEBUTED AT THE 132ND OAKS DAY IN 2006 AND WAS CREATED BY TIM LAIRD FOR CHURCHILL DOWNS AS THE FIRST SIGNATURE DRINK OF THIS PRESTIGIOUS RACE, RUN ON THE FRIDAY BEFORE DERBY DAY. THIS DRINK NOW RIVALS THE MINT JULEP. THE COLOR OF THE DRINK EMULATES THE STARGAZER LILY, WHICH IS THE FLOWER IN THE PRIZED BLANKET AWARDED TO THE WINNING HORSE OF THE OAKS RACE KNOWN AS THE "LILIES FOR THE FILLIES."

Thoroughbred Punch

½ cup sugar

4 ounces lemon juice

6 ounces orange juice

4 ounces grenadine

1 liter Woodford Reserve bourbon

1 liter club soda

1 bunch mint

Combine sugar, lemon juice and orange juice and stir well. Add grenadine and bourbon, then stir again. Add the club soda, ice block and serve over ice with mint sprigs.

Serves 15 – 18

Caviar

4 ounces Spoonfish or Paddlefish Caviar   2 tablespoons butter, softened
4 slices white bread, sliced thin

OPTIONAL GARNISHES
Red onion, diced
Hard-boiled egg yolk, diced
Hard-boiled egg white, diced
Capers, diced
Sour cream

Lightly toast the bread so it is still soft, not crumbly like crackers. Spread one side with butter, cut off the crusts and cut diagonally twice so you end up with 4 mini-triangles of toast. Repeat with the remaining pieces of bread.

Let your guests build their own toasts as they wish, with just the plain caviar (our recommendation) or with the optional garnishes.

Serves 6

NOTE: WE RECOMMEND SPOONFISH OR PADDLEFISH CAVIAR.

Tomato Sandwiches

12 slices white bread
5 Roma tomatoes, thinly sliced
1 cup mayonnaise

1 sweet onion, thinly sliced to fit bread
2 bunches Italian parsley, finely chopped

Cut 1 – 1½-inch rounds out of bread using a cookie cutter or top of jar. You should be able to get approximately 3 rounds per slice of bread. Spread mayonnaise on one side of each bread round. Place onion slice on bread round. Top with tomato slice. Top with second piece of bread. Spread a thin layer of mayonnaise around the outside edge of the sandwich. Place chopped parsley on a flat plate. Roll mayonnaise edge of the sandwich in chopped parsley.

Serves 6

Goat Cheese with Mint

12 ounces soft goat cheese, room temperature
3 tablespoons milk
2 teaspoons whole cumin seeds
1 teaspoon dried dill
½ teaspoon fresh ground black pepper

2 cloves garlic, crushed
2 tablespoons extra virgin olive oil
20 mint leaves, thinly sliced
Crackers

In a small bowl, combine the goat cheese, milk, cumin seeds, dill, black pepper and garlic. Cover and refrigerate for at least 1 hour. Flavor is best if made the night before. Transfer cheese to a platter, form into a mound, sprinkle with mint leaves, then drizzle with olive oil. Serve with crackers.

Serves 8

Kentucky Eggs Benedict

½ cup butter (1 stick), cut into
    tablespoon-size pieces
2 egg yolks
1 teaspoon fresh lemon juice
¼ cup boiling water
Dash salt

Dash cayenne pepper
6 thin slices country ham
2 tablespoons white vinegar
6 eggs
6 slices whole grain bread
Paprika

In the top of a double boiler, whisk egg yolks and lemon juice. Add 3 tablespoons of the butter. Place double boiler over simmering water. Cook, whisking constantly, until butter melts and sauce begins to thicken. Add 3 more tablespoons of butter, whisk until butter melts, then add remaining 2 tablespoons of butter. Slowly whisk in boiling water. Continue cooking over simmering water and whisking, until mixture thickens, about 2 – 3 minutes. Remove from heat. Stir in salt and cayenne pepper.

Place ham slices on rack of broiler pan. Broil 4 inches from heat for about 4 minutes, or until ham begins to brown.

While ham is broiling, pour about 3 inches of water into a pan. Add white vinegar and lightly salt the water. Bring to the boiling point. Carefully put eggs in the water, breaking into a cup first, then gently slipping them into the water one at a time.

Simmer eggs for 3 – 4 minutes or until set. Remove with slotted spoon, drain, pat dry with a dish or paper towel.

Lightly toast the bread and place on a serving plate. Top with a slice of ham and a poached egg. Spoon a little sauce over the egg and sprinkle with paprika. Serve immediately.

Serves 6

NOTE: EGGS CAN BE POACHED A DAY AHEAD OF TIME AND KEPT IN THE REFRIGERATOR IN A BOWL OF COLD WATER. REHEAT BEFORE SERVING BY DIPPING THEM IN A PAN OF SLIGHTLY BOILING WATER.

Grilled Asparagus

1 pound fresh asparagus, trimmed and peeled	1 teaspoon salt
4 tablespoons olive oil	Fresh ground pepper

Preheat grill to medium-high.

Drizzle olive oil over the asparagus and turn spears until they are coated. Sprinkle with salt and pepper. Grill for 5 minutes. Roll the asparagus from time-to-time so it browns evenly but does not char. Remove from grill and serve immediately.

Serves 6

NOTE: WHEN CHOOSING ASPARAGUS, LOOK FOR FIRM STALKS WITH FIRM DEEP GREEN OR PURPLISH TIPS. TRIM OFF THE TOUGH BOTTOM OF THE SPEAR BY GRASPING EACH END AND BENDING IT GENTLY UNTIL IT SNAPS AT ITS NATURAL POINT OF TENDERNESS, USUALLY $^2/_3$ OF THE WAY DOWN THE SPEAR. USING A VEGETABLE PEELER, PEEL OFF THE OUTER SKIN OF THE LOWER HALF OF THE REMAINING STALK.

Bison Stew

2 pounds buffalo cube steak or stew meat, cut into 1-inch cubes	¼ teaspoon dried oregano
¼ cup flour	¼ teaspoon dried basil
½ teaspoon salt	1 teaspoon Worcestershire sauce
½ teaspoon ground black pepper	1½ cups low sodium beef broth
2 cloves garlic, minced	¼ cup Old Forester bourbon
1 bay leaf	3 Idaho potatoes, peeled and diced
1 teaspoon paprika	4 carrots, peeled and sliced
¼ teaspoon dried thyme	1 stalk celery, chopped
	1 cup frozen pearl onions, thawed

Place meat in slow cooker. In a small bowl, mix together the flour, salt and pepper. Pour over the meat and stir to coat. Stir in the garlic, bay leaf, paprika, thyme, oregano, basil, Worcestershire sauce, beef broth, bourbon, potatoes, carrots, celery and pearl onions.

Cover and cook on low setting for 10 – 12 hours or on high setting for 4 – 6 hours.

Remove the bay leaf and serve over wide noodles, rice or with a chunk of crusty bread.

Serves 6

NOTE: DO NOT BE INTIMIDATED BY THE LONG LIST OF INGREDIENTS. THERE REALLY IS NOT MUCH WORK INVOLVED. JUST ADD EVERYTHING TO THE SLOW COOKER AND TURN IT ON.

Bluegrass Peaches with Ice Cream

3 peaches, halved and peeled
6 teaspoons brown sugar, separated
3 tablespoons butter, cut into 6 pieces
6 tablespoons Woodford Reserve bourbon,
   separated

6 dashes of cinnamon
6 scoops vanilla ice cream

Preheat oven to 350 degrees.

Cut peaches in half and core. Place on a baking sheet, cavity side up. Fill each cavity with: 1 teaspoon brown sugar, ½ tablespoon butter, 1 tablespoon bourbon and 1 dash of cinnamon. Bake until sauce is melted and peach is soft, approximately 10 – 15 minutes. Serve over scoop of ice cream.

Serves 6

Timeline

1 WEEK AHEAD
- Shop for non-perishable groceries
- Order caviar

2 DAYS AHEAD
- Shop for last-minute groceries
- Pick up caviar
- Make the Mint Simple Syrup

1 DAY AHEAD
- Make the garnishes for the caviar
- Make the goat cheese
- Clean the asparagus; store in zip-top plastic bag in refrigerator
- Poach the eggs
- Make pitchers of the Oaks Lily
- Make pitchers of Mint Juleps for Many
- Make the Thorougbred Punch (if serving)

MORNING OF THE PARTY
- Chop the mint for the Goat Cheese with Mint
- Cut out bread rounds for Tomato Sandwiches and store in zip-top plastic bag
- Slice Roma tomatoes
- Slice sweet onion
- Chop Italian parsley
- Prepare the Bison Stew
- Measure and portion the ingredients for the Bluegrass Peaches so you only have to assemble and bake when ready for dessert.

2 HOURS AHEAD
- Cut and toast the bread for the Caviar
- Make the sauce for the Kentucky Eggs Benedict

1 HOUR AHEAD
- Plate the Goat Cheese with Mint
- Grill and plate the asparagus; serve at room temperature
- Reheat the eggs and assemble the Kentucky Eggs Benedict
- Assemble and plate the Tomato Sandwiches; cover with plastic wrap until serving

JUST BEFORE THE PARTY
- Plate the Caviar
- Reheat the sauce for the Kentucky Eggs Benedict and pour over the eggs at the last minute
- Set out all food items
- Check bar; put ice in bucket; set out pitcher drinks, sodas and water

Shopping List

Spoonfish or Paddlefish Caviar
White bread, 1 loaf
Red onion, 1
Capers, 1 jar
Goat cheese, 12 ounces
Mint leaves, 2 bunches
Garlic, 1 bulb
Crackers
Roma tomatoes, 5
Sweet onion, 1
Italian parsley, 2 bunches
Asparagus, 1 pound
Eggs, 1 dozen
Country ham, 6 slices
Whole grain bread, 1 loaf
Buffalo cube steak or stew meat,
  2 pounds
Low sodium beef broth, 1 can
Idaho Potatoes, 3
Carrots, 4
Celery, 1 bunch
Frozen pearl onions, 1 bag
Peaches, 3
Vanilla ice cream
Blackberries, 1 pint
Lemons, 2
Sweet and sour mix
Cranberry juice
Old Forester bourbon
Woodford Reserve bourbon
Finlandia vodka
Triple sec
Grenadine

ALSO BUY, IF NOT
IN YOUR PANTRY

Unsalted butter
Sour cream
Milk
Cumin seeds
Dried dill
Black pepper
Salt
Extra virgin olive oil
Mayonnaise
Cayenne pepper
White vinegar
Paprika
Flour
Bay leaves
Dried thyme
Dried oregano
Dried basil
Worcestershire sauce
Brown sugar
Cinnamon
Sugar
Orange juice
Club soda

Brunch

Brunch

Brunch says it all…the best of breakfast and lunch, combined to make a great party for entertaining. Brunch can be celebrated anytime throughout the year and is commensurate with occasions such as Mother's Day, birthdays, graduations, bridal/baby showers and more. This can be an easy and affordable occasion and can be adapted for a small intimate group or a large party. Brunch themes can vary by using thematic music, linens and flower colors and party favors.

The beverages for brunch are traditionally mimosas and Bloody Marys. You can easily expand these categories to offer your guests an array of flavors by setting up champagne and Bloody Mary stations. Your guests can build their own with a wide selection of flavors and spices. We also offer alcohol-free sparklers by substituting lemon-lime soda for the champagne.

Since you have prepared all of your brunch dishes, we suggest you give yourself a break and purchase dessert. Great ideas include mini fruit tarts, bite-sized pecan pies, chocolate cups filled with Tuaca Italian liqueur, Chambord liqueur, or your favorite liqueur, petits fours and chocolate truffles.

Enjoy your brunch with a few close friends or turn it into an open house with a buffet. The options are endless.

OVER THE TOP BRUNCH IDEAS

- Set up a sushi station and hire your favorite sushi chef to make signature rolls and appetizers
- Hire a three-piece musical combo: jazz or classical to fit your theme
- Set up an omelet station and hire a chef to make personalized omelets
- Fly in special guests to surprise the guest of honor with family or friends they never expected to attend
- Hire a magician, fortune teller, handwriting analyst or caricature artist for added entertainment

THEME IDEAS

VALENTINE'S DAY

Music: Romantic

Linen and flower colors: Pinks and reds

Party favors: Individually boxed chocolate truffles

BIRTHDAY

Music: Decade of the guest of honor's favorite music ('50s, '60s, '70s and beyond)

Linen and flower colors: Guest of honor's favorite colors

Party favors: Individually packaged cupcakes

GRADUATION

Music: Top 40

Linen and flower colors: School colors

Party favors: Personalized plastic cups such as: "Susie Smith's Graduation Party! Class of 20XX" These can be used at the party, then taken home as a favor.

BRIDAL AND BABY SHOWERS

Music: Pop

Linen and flower colors: Wedding scheme colors, or pink, blue, green or yellow for baby showers

Party favors: White or pastel-colored Jordan Almonds, tied in tulle

MOTHER'S DAY

Music: Classical

Linen and flower colors: Mothers' and grandmothers' favorite colors

Party favors: Picture frames with family pictures

Mimosa Station

For a twist on the classic mimosa (champagne and orange juice), set out champagne and other juices so your guests can create their own signature mimosas.

Cranberry	Pear
Pomegranate	Mango
Guava	Pineapple
Peach	

NOTE: LEMON-LIME SODA CAN BE SUBSTITUTED FOR THE CHAMPAGNE FOR AN ALCOHOL-FREE MIMOSA. USE WINE GLASSES INSTEAD OF CHAMPAGNE GLASSES. THEY ARE MORE STABLE, EASIER TO DRINK FROM AND EASIER TO POUR INTO, ESPECIALLY WHEN ADDING JUICES AND OTHER MIXERS. IF YOU ADD A FEW POMEGRANATE SEEDS OR DRIED CRANBERRIES TO YOUR GLASS OF CHAMPAGNE, THEY WILL FLOAT UP AND DOWN LIKE A LAVA LAMP.

130

Bloody Mary Station

For a fun Bloody Mary station, set out a pitcher of basic tomato juice or Bloody Mary mix, along with vodka and any or all of the following garnishes. Your guests can build their own.

Horseradish	Olives stuffed with garlic or blue cheese
Steak sauce	Cooked and peeled shrimp
Finely grated parmesan or blue cheese	Hot sauce
Celery salt and celery stalks	Jalapeño peppers
Pickled mushrooms	Pepper flakes
Pickled asparagus spears	Balsamic vinegar
Pickled green beans	Lemon and lime wedges
Pickled green tomatoes	

NOTE: IN ADDITION TO VODKA, SET OUT A BOURBON ON YOUR BLOODY MARY BAR, AS IT GIVES A NICE TWIST TO THE STANDARD RECIPE.

Cajun Shrimp and Cucumber

1 pound frozen, raw shrimp, peeled and deveined (45-50 count)	Salt
	Black pepper
2 teaspoons extra virgin olive oil	1 English (seedless) cucumber, sliced into ¼-inch rounds
4 teaspoons Cajun seasoning	
4 teaspoons Southern Comfort	½ cup sour cream
Tabasco, several dashes (optional)	Paprika

Defrost the shrimp according to directions on the package. Marinate the shrimp in the olive oil, Cajun seasoning, Southern Comfort and Tabasco for 10 minutes. Sauté in a hot pan until cooked through and just pink and opaque in color, approximately 3 – 4 minutes. Season to taste with salt and pepper. Place a dollop of sour cream on a slice of cucumber and top with a cooked shrimp. Repeat with the remaining cucumber, sour cream and shrimp. Garnish with a dusting of paprika.

Serves 10 – 12

SoCo Nuts

2 tablespoons butter	4 cups raw nuts (almonds, walnuts, pecans)
2 tablespoons brown sugar	Kosher salt
2 ounces Southern Comfort	

Preheat oven to 200 degrees.

In a small pan, melt the butter and brown sugar. Add the Southern Comfort and heat to combine. In a bowl with the nuts, add the glaze and toss. Spread in a single layer on a baking sheet. Bake for 20 minutes. Sprinkle with Kosher salt to taste. Serve warm or at room temperature.

Makes 4 cups

Melon, Prosciutto and Mozzarella Skewers

1 small (about 2-pound) cantaloupe, halved
   crosswise, seeded, cut into 20 wedges
10 small fresh water-packed
   mozzarella balls

10 thin slices of prosciutto, cut in half
   lengthwise, gathered into ruffle
10 8-inch skewers

Cut each cantaloupe wedge crosswise in half. Each skewer should include 1 melon piece, 1 ruffled prosciutto piece, 1 mozzarella ball, 1 prosciutto piece and 1 melon piece. Repeat with remaining skewers. Can be prepared 2 hours ahead of time. Cover and refrigerate. Bring to room temperature 15 minutes before serving.

Arrange skewers on platter or poke into a melon half.

Serves 10

Roasted Red Pepper Frittata

2 tablespoons olive oil	2 tablespoons chives, finely chopped
1 teaspoon salt	2 teaspoons fresh basil leaves, finely chopped
½ teapsoon fresh ground black pepper	12 eggs, beaten
2 tablespoons fresh parsley leaves, finely chopped	½ cup sliced roasted red peppers, seeded
	¾ cup crumbled goat cheese

Preheat oven to 350 degrees.

In a large bowl, add the eggs, salt, pepper, parsley, chives and basil and beat well. In an oven-proof non-stick skillet, add the oil, heat to medium-high heat. Pour the egg mixture into the hot skillet, reduce the heat to medium and cook about 4 minutes. Add the roasted red peppers and goat cheese to the top of the frittata. Put in the oven and cook until the center is set, about 12 – 15 minutes. Let cool and slide onto a serving platter. Slice into wedges and serve.

Serves 10 – 12

CUSTOMIZE YOUR FRITTATA

You can customize your frittata based on your preferences and brunch theme. Follow the same cooking directions but substitute any combination of the below for the goat cheese and roasted red pepper.

VEGETABLES AND MEATS (Choose any combination for a total of 1 cup)

Asparagus, steamed, cut into 1-inch pieces

Potatoes, peeled, boiled, cut into ¼-inch thick slices

Mushrooms of any variety, cut into ¼-inch slices, sautéed

Italian sausage crumbled, cooked

Onions, thinly sliced, sautéed

Pancetta or bacon, cooked, diced

Spinach chopped, sautéed, squeezed dry

CHEESE OPTIONS (choose 1 or 2 for up to a total of ¾ cup)

Feta, crumbled

Fresh ricotta in dollops

Grated Parmigiano-Reggiano

Fontina, shredded

FRESH HERB OPTIONS

Basil, finely chopped

Chives, finely chopped

Parsley, finely chopped

Oregano, finely chopped

Maple-Glazed Bacon

1 pound bacon, thick cut	½ cup maple syrup

Preheat oven to 400 degrees.

Place bacon on a baking sheet. Bake in oven for 10 minutes. Remove from oven and brush generously with maple syrup. Return pan to oven for 5 minutes or desired doneness. Transfer bacon to paper bag to drain. Place on platter, serve immediately.

Serves 10

Bourbon Pork Tenderloin on a Baguette

¼ cup Woodford Reserve bourbon	1 teaspoon Worcestershire sauce
¼ cup soy sauce	¼ cup vegetable oil
¼ cup brown sugar, packed	2 1-pound pork tenderloins
3 cloves garlic, minced	1 baguette, sliced
¼ cup Dijon mustard	Dijon mustard
1 teaspoon fresh ginger, minced or	Roasted red peppers, seeded,
¼ teaspoon powdered ginger	sliced into 20 strips

Combine bourbon, soy sauce, brown sugar, garlic, mustard, ginger, Worcestershire sauce and vegetable oil in a large bowl. Whisk until brown sugar has dissolved. Set aside ½ cup for basting. Place marinade and pork tenderloins in a zip-top plastic bag and place in the refrigerator overnight. Bring to room temperature. Grill over medium-high heat or bake at 350 degrees for approximately 15 – 25 minutes. Baste often while cooking. Pork should reach 165 degrees internally.

To serve: Spread mustard on baguette slice, top with pork tenderloin slice and roasted red pepper strip.

Serves 10 – 12

Cedar Plank Salmon

1 cedar plank (made for cooking, soaked in cold water for 20 minutes to 2 hours)	Salt
	Pepper
	½ cup maple syrup
1 3-4-pound top half of salmon	

Preheat grill to medium-high.

Remove the plank from the water and place on the grill for 3 minutes per side until it begins to smoke. Place salmon on plank, skin side down. Season with salt and pepper. Drizzle salmon with maple syrup. Cook for approximately 20 minutes or to medium-well doneness. Serve salmon on plank on platter.

Serves 10 – 12

NOTE: WATCH TO MAKE SURE THE PLANK DOES NOT CATCH FIRE. IF IT DOES, MIST WITH A WATER BOTTLE. PLANK CAN BE RINSED, WASHED AND USED MULTIPLE TIMES.

Timeline

1 WEEK AHEAD
- Shop for non-perishable groceries
- Determine the theme of your brunch and buy or make the party favors

2 DAYS AHEAD
- Determine where you will set up your Bloody Mary Bar, Mimosa Bar, brunch buffet and dessert area

1 DAY AHEAD
- Shop for last-minute groceries
- Make the marinade for the Bourbon Pork Tenderloin on a Baguette and marinate the pork
- Clean all of the fresh herbs for the Roasted Red Pepper Frittata

MORNING OF THE PARTY
- Put all the garnishes and juices for the beverage bars in serving pitchers, bowls and glasses; refrigerate
- Cut the cantaloupe and prosciutto for the Melon, Prosciutto and Mozzarella Skewers

2 HOURS AHEAD
- Cook the shrimp and slice the cucumber for the Cajun Shrimp and Cucumber; refrigerate
- Assemble and plate the Melon, Prosciutto and Mozzarella Skewers; refrigerate

1 HOUR AHEAD
- Make the SoCo Nuts
- Set up the Bloody Mary Bar and Mimosa Bar
- Make and plate the Cedar Plank Salmon
- Cook the pork tenderloin; when cool, assemble and plate the Bourbon Pork Tenderloin on a Baguette
- Make and plate the Roasted Red Pepper Frittata
- Make and plate the SoCo Nuts
- Set out your dessert items

JUST BEFORE THE PARTY
- Make the Maple-Glazed Bacon
- Assemble and plate the Cajun Shrimp and Cucumber
- Set out all food items
- Put ice in bucket; set out the champagne

Shopping List

Bloody Mary mix or
  tomato juice
Finlandia vodka
Korbel champagne
Optional Garnishes:
  Horseradish
  Steak sauce
  Parmesan cheese
  Blue cheese
  Celery salt
  Celery
  Pickled mushrooms
  Pickled asparagus spears
  Pickled green beans
  Pickled green tomatoes
  Olives stuffed with garlic
    or blue cheese
  Cooked and peeled shrimp
  Hot sauce
  Jalapeño peppers
  Lemon
  Limes
Optional Juices:
  Cranberry juice
  Pomegranate juice
  Guava juice
  Peach juice
  Pear juice
  Mango juice
  Pineapple juice
Raw shrimp, 1 pound, frozen,
  peeled, deveined
  (45-50 count)
Southern Comfort
English (seedless) cucumber, 1
Sour cream
Raw nuts — almonds, walnuts,
  pecans, 4 cups
Cantaloupe, 1 small,
  about 2 pounds
Mozzarella balls, 10 small,
  fresh water-packed
Prosciutto, 10 thin slices
Fresh parsley, 1 bunch
Fresh chives, 1 bunch
Fresh basil, 1 bunch
Eggs, 1 dozen
Roasted red peppers, 1 jar

Goat cheese, crumbled,
  1 small container
Bacon, 1 pound, thick slices
Woodford Reserve bourbon
Pork tenderloins, 2 1-pound
Garlic, 1 bulb
Baguette, 1
Cedar plank, made for
  cooking, 1
Salmon fillet, 1 3-4-pound
Mini fruit tarts
Bite-sized pecan pies
Chocolate cups
Petits Fours
Chocolate Truffles
Tuaca Italian liqueur
Chambord liqueur
Old Forester bourbon

ALSO BUY, IF NOT IN YOUR PANTRY

Extra virgin olive oil
Balsamic Vinegar
Cajun seasoning
Tabasco (optional)
Kosher salt
Pepper
Paprika
Butter
Brown sugar
8-inch skewers, 10
Maple syrup
Soy sauce
Dijon mustard
Ginger — fresh or powdered
Worcestershire sauce
Vegetable oil

Pizza Party

Everyone loves pizza and grilling. I have put these two passions together and created a grilled pizza party. Once you have experienced pizza on the grill, you will not have it any other way. You will be amazed how easy it is to make your own dough and how light, thin and crispy it gets when you grill it. Not only does grilling give the pies a smoky flavor, it also keeps your house cool by not having to heat up your oven in the kitchen. Grilled pizzas are easy to make and inexpensive, thus making this a perfect party to invite lots of friends, family and neighbors.

The secret is getting everyone involved in the act. Most guests like to help and it gives them a sense of contribution. Assign duties to your guests and let them play host as well. Find out your guests' passions and expertise, then let them shine. For example, there are many who like to play bartender or have specialty dishes they like to bring and show off. This is extreme, but I once hosted a party and assigned a dish to everyone and only provided the location, beverages and serving pieces. This works especially well with a pizza party where guests bring their favorite toppings. Others can participate by rolling dough, cutting and serving.

Nothing goes better with pizza than Italian varietal wines like Chianti and pinot grigio. These are also very affordable. Like they do in Italy, I serve these wines in little shell or juice glasses. Forget the stemware, as this is casual pizza fun.

Finally, for dessert, set up a coffee, Tuaca and biscotti bar. Tuaca is a vanilla-based Italian liqueur and is enjoyed over ice, in a cordial glass or in coffee. The biscotti is a perfect ending as it provides a little sweetness and crunch to go along with your coffee, with or without the Tuaca.

TIPS AND HINTS
- To save time, buy your pizza toppings from your grocer's salad bar. Here you will find pre-chopped mushrooms, onions and green peppers ready to use.
- Vegetables for the antipasto can be chopped one day ahead and stored in individual containers in the refrigerator.

- Mushrooms – Pan-sear these ahead of time, taking out the water to avoid making the pizza soggy.
- Sausage – Roll the sausage pieces in flour and pan-sear ahead of time. This cuts down on the grease.
- Cheese – For a healthier option, or for those who are lactose intolerant, try lactose-free mozzarella found in most grocery stores with the other shredded cheeses.
- Roll dough early the morning of the party. Place each on a sheet of parchment paper, sprinkle with cornmeal, stack in layers (no more than 4) and store in the refrigerator.
- Watch your dough so it does not burn on the bottom. You will quickly determine the proper heat setting for your grill, whether you use gas or charcoal.
- Do not overload your pizza with too many toppings as the weight will cause your pie to get soggy and will be hard to remove from the grill. Simplicity is the key to these pies.
- Throw a few wood chips on the charcoal or gas flames to add a smoky taste to your pies.
- Because of the crispy crusts, leftover pizzas can be easily frozen in zip-top plastic bags and reheated in the oven.

PIZZA COMBINATIONS / TOPPING IDEAS
- Olive oil with caramelized onions, blue cheese, rosemary sprigs
- Pesto sauce with chicken, mozzarella cheese (Buy the rotisserie cooked chicken, remove the skin and shred.)
- Tomato sauce with goat cheese, basil
- Barbecue chicken pizza – your favorite barbecue sauce, grilled chicken, diced green onions, mozzarella cheese
- Crisp bacon, onion, smoked mozzarella cheese
- Pesto with shrimp, roasted red and yellow peppers
- Roasted eggplant, sweet peppers, caramelized onions, mozzarella cheese
- Olive oil with fresh mozzarella, sliced tomatoes, Parmigiano-Reggiano cheese, basil

GRILLING TIPS
- Do not be in a hurry to turn.
- Once you place your dough on the grill, leave it alone until it is time to flip it. This is usually 3 – 4 minutes, depending on the heat of your grill.
- Keep a lid on it. Every time you look under the lid, you lose heat and smoke, which gives your pizza that grilled flavor.
- Keep your grates seasoned by brushing the grates with oil after each use.

Tuscan Twist

3 ounces Tuaca Italian liqueur	1 ounce orange liqueur
6 ounces lemonade	

In a shaker with ice, add the Tuaca, lemonade and orange liqueur. Shake and strain into glasses with ice. Garnish with lemon twists.

Serves 2

TO MAKE BY THE PITCHER

This recipe can be made by the part:

1 part Tuaca Italian liqueur

2 parts lemonade

⅓ part orange liqueur

Stir and serve over ice. Garnish with lemon slices.

For an alcohol-free version, omit the Tuaca and orange liqueur, and replace them with orange juice. Stir and pour over ice with lemon garnish.

Antipasto

2 red peppers, sliced

2 yellow peppers, sliced

1 large bunch asparagus,
  3-inch spears, blanched

25 fresh small mozzarella balls, drained

1 14-ounce can quartered artichoke hearts

25 pimento-stuffed olives

1 pound pepperoni or summer sausage,
  cubed

Vinaigrette:

⅓ cup cider vinegar

¼ cup fresh parsley, finely chopped

2 tablespoons extra virgin olive oil

2 teaspoons oregano, dried

1 teaspoon sugar

¼ teaspoon salt

¼ teaspoon black pepper

3 cloves garlic, crushed

Whisk the vinegar, parsley, olive oil, oregano, sugar, salt, pepper and garlic. Toss the vegetables, cheese and meat with the vinaigrette. Marinate for a minimum of 2 hours in the refrigerator before serving.

Serves 10 – 12

Grilled Pizzas

DOUGH

4 cups flour	2 tablespoons olive oil
1 teaspoon salt	1½ cups warm water (120 to 130 degrees)
1 teaspoon sugar	Cooking spray
2 packages quick-rise yeast	4 tablespoons cornmeal

Combine the flour, salt, sugar, yeast, oil and water in a large food processor or stand mixer. Mix until dough forms a ball, 4 – 5 minutes.

Place the dough in a large bowl coated with cooking spray, turning to coat top. Cover with a kitchen towel and let rise in a warm place, free from drafts, 45 minutes or until doubled in size. Punch the dough down. Cover and let it rest for 10 more minutes.

Divide the dough into 4 – 5 equal-sized balls. Working with one ball at a time (cover remaining dough to keep from drying out), roll into a 10-inch circle on a lightly floured surface. Place dough on a pizza pan sprinkled with 1 tablespoon cornmeal. Repeat with remaining dough.

Makes 4 – 5 10-inch pizzas

SAUCE

28-ounce can crushed tomatoes	2 tablespoons sugar
4 cloves garlic, crushed	

Pour crushed tomatoes into a large bowl and add the garlic and sugar. Stir well and store in the refrigerator until ready to use. Use a large ladle to pour onto the crust. The back of the ladle works well to help move the sauce evenly over the crust.

GRILLING THE PIZZAS

Preheat the grill to medium heat. Place doughs on the clean grill grates for 2 – 3 minutes. (Most grills will accommodate two or more pizzas.) Check to make sure they have browned slightly.

Flip the doughs, brush with olive oil, then top with sauce (if using one), toppings and, finally, cheese.

Grill with lid down another 15 – 20 minutes or until cheese has melted. Check the bottom of the crusts periodically to make sure they do not burn.

Timeline

1 WEEK AHEAD
- Shop for non-perishable groceries
- Set up wine bar

1 DAY AHEAD
- Shop for last-minute groceries
- Chop vegetables for Antipasto
- Make vinaigrette for Antipasto

MORNING OF THE PARTY
- Make the dough
- Make the tomato sauce
- Make the signature cocktail, Tuscan Twist
- Place the pizza toppings in individual bowls for easy access
- Set up biscotti bar

4 HOURS AHEAD
- Roll the dough; refrigerate
- Toss the Antipasto

JUST BEFORE THE PARTY
- Plate the Antipasto
- Take out the pizza ingredients and arrange them near the grill
- Make coffee; put in thermos
- Check bar; fill ice buckets; set out garnishes
- Preheat grill

Shopping List

Quick rise yeast, 2 packages
   per dough recipe
28-ounce can crushed tomatoes
Garlic, 1 bulb
Onions, 2
Blue cheese
Fresh rosemary sprigs
Pesto sauce
Cooked chicken
Shredded mozzarella cheese
Goat cheese
Basil, 1 bunch
Red peppers, 2
Yellow peppers, 2
Asparagus, 1 bunch
Small mozzarella balls, (fresh), 25
14-ounce can quartered
   artichoke hearts
pimento stuffed olives, 1 jar
Pepperoni or summer sausage,
   1 pound
Italian parsley, 1 bunch
Lemonade
Orange liqueur
Tuaca Italian liqueur
Chianti
Pinot grigio
Biscotti

ALSO BUY, IF NOT IN YOUR PANTRY

Flour
Salt
Sugar
Olive oil
Cooking spray
Cornmeal
Cider vinegar
Dried oregano
Black pepper

Fourth of July

Independence Day is a birthday party like none other. Whether you celebrate with family or your entire block, the Fourth of July is always a blast, and it is the perfect time to throw a colorful outdoor party.

Before your patriotic patrons gather to watch the skies fill with fireworks, put on a show of your own with a Fourth of July menu that explodes with color and flavor.

You can throw a party that looks and even tastes like the Fourth of July.

Since it is summer, heat it up with spicy foods and cool it down with fun frozen cocktails and Bomb Pops.

Nobody will forget the Fourth at your house after experiencing Firecracker Shrimp, Red, White and Blue Burgers and even adult Sparklers.

Korbel Sparklers

FOR BLUE

In a white wine glass, add Korbel champagne and enough Blue Curacao until desired color is achieved.

FOR WHITE

In a white wine glass, add Korbel champagne.

FOR RED

In a white wine glass, add Korbel champagne and cranberry juice until desired color is achieved.

FOURTH OF JULY

Red, White and Blue Daiquiris

Purchase strawberry daiquiri and pina colada mixers. I recommend the Finest Call brand, as they make some of the best mixers I have tasted. This will be the base for your red and white layers. Follow the directions on the bottle for the blender/frozen version using Finlandia mango vodka or Southern Comfort. For the blue layer, blend ice and Blue Curacao or a blue raspberry mixer and the spirit of your choice. Once frozen, put the blue layer on the bottom, then the white layer, and top with the red. Add a straw and enjoy.

NOTE: TO MAKE AN ALCOHOL-FREE VERSION, SIMPLY LEAVE OUT THE SPIRITS AND BUILD AS SUGGESTED ABOVE.

Firecracker Shrimp

1 pound raw jumbo shrimp, frozen (20 count), cleaned and deveined	1 teaspoon fresh ground ginger
1 cup Frank's Red Hot Sauce	1 teaspoon fresh lemon juice
1 tablespoon olive oil	20 fresh rosemary sprigs
4 cloves garlic, crushed	Sriracha hot sauce

Defrost the shrimp according to directions on the package. Remove the tails from the shrimp and place the shrimp in a small bowl with the hot sauce. Mix to combine. Set aside.

In a medium-size sauté pan, over medium-high heat, add the oil, garlic and ginger. Cook for 2 minutes, until soft. Add the lemon juice and shrimp with the hot sauce and cook for about 3 minutes, until the shrimp are cooked through. Skewer each shrimp with a rosemary spear and serve immediately. Garnish with a dot of Sriracha at the base of the rosemary spear.

Serves 4 – 6

Red, White and Blue Chips with Pico de Gallo

1½ cups tomatoes, seeded and diced
½ cup white onion, diced
2 tablespoons jalapeños, diced
Juice of 1 lime

Kosher salt
Fresh ground black pepper
2 tablespoons cilantro, finely chopped

In a medium-size bowl, combine the tomatoes, white onion, jalapeños and lime juice. Season with salt and pepper to taste. Just before serving, mix in the cilantro.

Serve with red, white and blue tortilla chips.

Makes 2 cups

Red, White and Blue Bean Salad

1 15-ounce can cannellini beans,
   rinsed and drained
1 15-ounce can kidney beans,
   rinsed and drained
1 15-ounce can black beans,
   rinsed and drained
½ red onion, finely chopped
2 tablespoons fresh flat-leaf parsley,
   finely chopped

2 tablespoons fresh cilantro, finely chopped
2 tablespoons olive oil
2 tablespoons apple cider vinegar
1 tablespoon sugar
½ teaspoon salt
½ teaspoon fresh ground black pepper

In a large bowl, combine the three types of beans, red onion, parsley and cilantro. In a separate small bowl, whisk together the oil, vinegar, sugar, salt and pepper. Pour the dressing over the beans and toss to coat well. Refrigerate for a minimum of 2 hours for the flavors to combine.

Serves 4 – 6

Red, White and Blue Burgers

2 pounds lean ground beef
½ white onion, finely chopped
1 teaspoon soy sauce
1 teaspoon Worcestershire sauce
2 cloves garlic, crushed
1 teaspoon dried parsley
1 teaspoon dried basil

1 teaspoon dried oregano
1 teaspoon black pepper
1 pinch mustard powder
16 hamburger "slider" buns
8 ounces blue cheese, formed into
   16 ½-ounce patties
4 Roma tomatoes, sliced

Preheat grill to high heat.

In a large bowl, mix the ground beef, onion, soy sauce, Worcestershire sauce, garlic, parsley, basil, oregano, pepper and mustard powder until combined. Form into 16 2-ounce patties. Grill patties for 3 – 4 minutes per side on the hot grill or until well done. Serve on buns with a slice of tomato and blue cheese.

Serves 4 – 6

NOTE: SINCE NOT EVERYONE LIKES BLUE CHEESE, YOU MIGHT WANT TO LEAVE IT OFF SOME OF THE BURGERS AND OFFER IT ON THE SIDE.

Red, White and Blue Parfait

To make this festive dessert, simply layer blueberries on the bottom of your serving bowl, then whipped cream, and top with sliced strawberries and raspberries. This can also be made in individual cups for easy serving.

Timeline

1 WEEK AHEAD
- Shop for non-perishable groceries
- Shop for Fourth of July decorations

2 DAYS AHEAD
- Plan your festive Fourth table with platters and serving pieces

1 DAY AHEAD
- Shop for last-minute groceries
- Make sure you have plenty of ice or buy, if necessary
- Put the shrimp in the refrigerator to defrost

MORNING OF THE PARTY
- Chill the champagne
- Make the Red, White and Blue Bean Salad
- Wash the fruit for the Red, White and Blue Parfait

2 HOURS AHEAD
- Make the Pico de Gallo
- Make the Red, White and Blue Burgers; refrigerate the patties until ready to cook
- Slice the Roma tomatoes for the burgers
- Make the blue cheese patties for the burgers; refrigerate

1 HOUR AHEAD
- Plate the Red, White and Blue Bean Salad

JUST BEFORE THE PARTY
- Make and freeze the layers for the daiquiris; build as your guests arrive
- Set out the mixers for the Korbel Sparklers
- Plate the Pico de Gallo and chips
- Make and plate the Firecracker Shrimp
- Cook the burgers for the Red, White and Blue Burgers and assemble
- Set out all other food items

WHEN READY TO SERVE DESSERT
- Assemble the Red, White and Blue Parfait
- Set out the Bomb Pops

Shopping List

Tomatoes, 3
White onion, 1
Jalapeños, 1 jar
Cilantro, 1 bunch
Lime, 1
Red, white and blue tortilla chips
Frozen raw jumbo shrimp,
   1 pound (20 count),
    peeled and deveined
Frank's Red Hot Sauce, 1 bottle
Garlic bulb, 1
Ginger, 1 knob
Lemon, 1
Fresh Rosemary, 1 bunch
Sriracha hot sauce
Cannellini beans, 1 15-ounce can
Kidney beans, 1 15-ounce can
Black beans, 1 15-ounce can
Red onion, 1
Fresh flat-leaf parsley, 1 bunch
Apple cider vinegar
Lean ground beef, 2 pounds
Hamburger "slider" buns, 16
Blue cheese, 8 ounces
Roma tomatoes, 4
Blueberries
Strawberries
Raspberries
Whipped Cream
Bomb Pops
Korbel champagne
Blue Curacao
Cranberry juice
Pina Colada mix
Strawberry Daiquiri mix
Finlandia mango vodka or
   Southern Comfort

ALSO BUY, IF NOT IN YOUR PANTRY
Olive oil
Kosher salt
Black pepper
Sugar
Soy sauce
Worcestershire sauce
Dried parsley
Dried basil
Dried oregano
Mustard powder

Party to Go

Take the party with you wherever you go. Whether planning a picnic, trip to the beach, concert in the park or any other outdoor event, you can bring the party along. The key to a Party to Go is to stay mobile, light and offer an assortment of food to please everyone. Another consideration is preparing items which will keep well in coolers, require few utensils and need little to no set-up once you arrive at your location.

TIPS

*   Buy a good cooler that is light, sturdy and portable. There are many available with wheels and retractable handles.
*   Pack an assortment of food items which will appeal to all tastes.
*   Consider foods that keep well with little cooling; skip the mayonnaise.
*   Lighten your load by converting glass to Lucite or plastic. You can pour a bottle of wine or mixed cocktails into a plastic bottle and not have to worry about corkscrews or anything else, as it will easily seal and reseal as needed. Lucite wine glasses give you the feel of an elegant glass without the worry of breakage.
*   Pack side items in individual disposable containers for easy serving and clean-up.
*   Use gel freezer packs to keep things cool. Place inside of a zip-top plastic bag to protect from leaks and remember to place the gel packs on top of your food in the cooler.
*   Pack a small, light foldable table and include items to dress up your Party to Go simply and elegantly. This includes a small blanket, tablecloth and even candles and flowers. Instead of packing a vase, use a plastic water bottle.

That's a wrap! Wrap sandwiches are easy to make and eat. They are versatile and usually hold up better than bread when you're on the move. There are many choices of wraps, from whole-grain, wheat, spinach, plain, tomato and more. For the inside, there are no limits. Make a variety to suit all takers. This could include an assortment of roasted vegetables, turkey breast, cheeses and roast beef. Cut into halves, wrap in plastic, and identify each with a marker.

Include light and nutritious sides you can eat with just a fork. Pack individual disposable soufflé cups with a selection of oil and vinegar cole slaw, pasta salad and seasoned brown rice.

For dessert, try fresh fruit with a riesling sauce on the side. If you follow these tips, your Party to Go will be a delicious adventure!

Lynchburg Lemonade

In a tall glass, add:
2 ounces Jack Daniel's Tennessee Whiskey
2 ounces triple sec
2 ounces sweet and sour mix
8 ounces lemon-lime soda

Stir and serve over ice. Garnish with lemon slices.

Serves 2

For pitcher drinks or larger quantities, this recipe can be made by the part:

1 part Jack Daniel's Tennessee Whiskey
1 part triple sec
1 part sweet and sour mix
4 parts lemon-lime soda

Stir and serve over ice. Garnish with a lemon slices.

Brown Rice Salad

1 cup brown rice
½ cup Italian salad dressing
2 cups (2½ ounces) fresh spinach leaves, chopped
1 cup celery, chopped

½ cup walnuts, toasted and chopped
½ cup (1 bunch) green onions, chopped
1 teaspoon black pepper
½ teaspoon salt

Cook 1 cup of brown rice according to the directions on the package. In a large bowl, toss the warm rice with the salad dressing. Let cool in the refrigerator, then add the spinach, celery, walnuts, green onions, pepper and salt. Toss, cover and refrigerate until ready to serve. Can be made 2 hours ahead.

Serves 4 – 6

Pasta Salad

½ pound farfalle (bow-tie) pasta
1 14-ounce can quartered artichoke hearts,
   well-drained
1 14-ounce can hearts of palm, drained,
   cut into 1-inch pieces
2 cups cooked edamame (baby soybeans),
   shelled
20 cherry tomatoes, sliced in half

10 large green olives, sliced in half
3 tablespoons red wine vinegar
2 tablespoons olive oil
1 teaspoon Dijon mustard
¼ teaspoon salt
¼ teaspoon black pepper
2 tablespoons fresh basil, chopped

Cook the pasta according to the directions on the package. Rinse under cold water to cool and drain well. In a large bowl, toss the pasta with the artichoke hearts, hearts of palm, edamame, cherry tomatoes and green olives. In a small jar, add the red wine vinegar, olive oil, mustard, salt and pepper. Shake to combine. Before serving, toss the dressing with the pasta, vegetables and fresh basil.

Serves 4 – 6

Cole Slaw

1 12-ounce bag broccoli slaw (broccoli, carrots, red cabbage)	¼ cup fig-infused vinegar
1 red pepper, sliced lengthwise	¼ cup apple cider vinegar
½ sweet onion, sliced lengthwise	2 teaspoons dry mustard
½ cup sugar	2 teaspoons celery seed
⅓ cup vegetable oil	½ teaspoon salt

In a large bowl, combine the broccoli slaw, red pepper and onion.

In a small saucepan over medium heat, add the sugar, vegetable oil, fig-infused vinegar, cider vinegar, dry mustard, celery seed and salt. Raise the heat and bring to a boil, simmer until the sugar is dissolved, about 3 – 5 minutes. Pour over the vegetables and toss. Cover and refrigerate until cold.

Serves 4 – 6

NOTE: IF YOU CANNOT FIND THE BROCCOLI SLAW, YOU CAN CHOP A HEAD OF CABBAGE, RED CABBAGE, NAPA CABBAGE OR ANY COMBINATION OF THESE AND ADD SHREDDED CARROTS. IF YOU CANNOT FIND FIG-INFUSED VINEGAR, USE ALL APPLE CIDER VINEGAR.

Wrap Sandwiches

Remember to leave the mayonnaise at home and use mustards and oil and vinegar-based dressings to season your wraps. Here are a few great combinations:

- Spinach wrap with Roasted Red Pepper and Artichoke Salad and lettuce
- Whole wheat wrap with roast beef, horseradish cheese, lettuce and yellow mustard
- Tomato wrap with turkey, hummus, red onion, pepper jack cheese, lettuce and tomato
- Whole-grain wrap with roasted vegetables, tossed in oil and vinegar
- Plain wrap with ham, cheddar cheese and Dijon mustard

NOTE: IF YOU ARE IN A HURRY, ORDER YOUR FAVORITE WRAPS FROM THE DELI OR MARKET AND PACKAGE THEM IN INDIVIDUAL PORTIONS TO TAKE WITH YOU.

Roasted Red Pepper and Artichoke Salad

1 14-ounce can quartered artichoke hearts, well-drained	4 cloves garlic
1 7-ounce jar roasted red peppers, well-drained and seeded	2 tablespoons olive oil
	2 tablespoons fresh lemon juice
½ cup fresh parsley, stems removed	Kosher salt
¼ cup capers, well-drained	Ground black pepper

In a food processor, combine the artichoke hearts, roasted red peppers, parsley, capers, garlic, olive oil and lemon juice. Process using on/off turns until well-combined. Do not purée. Season to taste with salt and pepper, cover and refrigerate. This is best made 1 day ahead of time.

Makes 1¼ cups

NOTE: THIS IS GREAT AS A SALAD IN A WRAP, AS A DIP WITH PITA CHIPS OR TOSSED WITH WARM PASTA.

Fruitinis with Riesling Sauce

1½ cups cantaloupe, cut into small pieces	1 cup riesling wine
1½ cups blueberries	¼ cup sugar
1½ cups raspberries	Lemon zest, 4 3-inch long strips
1 kiwi, sliced	Plastic martini glasses

In a small saucepan, combine the wine, sugar and lemon zest. Bring to a boil and simmer until the sugar has dissolved and the sauce has reduced, about 8 – 10 minutes. Let cool on the stovetop. Pour into a plastic bottle with a sealable lid to transport.

To build your Fruitinis, put ¼ cup of the cantaloupe in a pie-shaped section of the martini glass. Repeat with the blueberries and raspberries. Garnish with a kiwi slice. Just before serving, pour the riesling sauce over the top of the fruit.

Serves 4 – 6

Timeline

1 WEEK AHEAD
- SHOP FOR NON-PERISHABLE GROCERIES

2 DAYS AHEAD
- IF BUYING YOUR WRAP SANDWICHES, CALL TO ORDER THEM FROM YOUR DELI OR MARKET
- PREPARE YOUR PICNIC BASKET OR COOLER BY MAKING A LIST OF ITEMS TO BRING AND ORGANIZING ITEMS YOU WILL NEED TO PACK (BLANKET, GARBAGE BAG, TABLECLOTH, FLOWERS, CANDLES, ETC.)
- MAKE SURE YOU HAVE PLENTY OF GEL ICE PACKS OR BAGS OF ICE IN THE FREEZER

1 DAY AHEAD
- SHOP FOR LAST-MINUTE GROCERIES
- MAKE THE ROASTED RED PEPPER AND ARTICHOKE SALAD
- MAKE THE RIESLING SAUCE FOR THE FRUITINIS WITH RIESLING SAUCE
- MAKE THE LYNCHBURG LEMONADE
- PACK YOUR VEHICLE WITH ALL OF THE NON-PERISHABLE ITEMS

MORNING OF THE PARTY TO GO
- MAKE THE PASTA SALAD
- MAKE THE COLE SLAW
- CUT THE FRUIT FOR THE FRUITINIS WITH RIESLING SAUCE
- SLICE THE LEMON GARNISHES FOR THE LYNCHBURG LEMONADE

2 HOURS AHEAD
- MAKE THE BROWN RICE SALAD

1 HOUR AHEAD
- MAKE AND PACKAGE YOUR WRAP SANDWICHES
- BUILD AND PACKAGE THE FRUITINIS WITH RIESLING SAUCE
- PACKAGE THE SIDE ITEMS INTO INDIVIDUAL TO-GO CONTAINERS

JUST BEFORE DEPARTING
- PACK THE COOLER WITH ALL OF THE FOOD AND BEVERAGES

Shopping List

Desired wraps and wrap ingredients
Quartered artichoke hearts,
  2 14-ounce cans
Roasted red peppers, 1 7-ounce jar
Fresh parsley, 1 bunch
Capers, 1 bottle
Garlic, 1 bulb
Lemons, 2
Broccoli slaw, 1 12-ounce bag
Red pepper, 1
Sweet onion, 1
Fig-infused vinegar
Farfalle (bow-tie) pasta, 1 box
Hearts of palm, 1 14-ounce can
Frozen edamame (baby soybeans),
  1 10-ounce bag, shelled
Cherry tomatoes, 1 pint
Large green olives, 1 jar
Fresh basil, 1 bunch
Brown rice, 1 bag
Italian salad dressing, 1 bottle
Fresh spinach leaves, 1 bag
Celery, 1 bunch
Walnuts, 1 small bag
Green onions, 1 bunch
Cantaloupe, 1
Blueberries
Raspberries
Kiwi, 1
Riesling wine
Plastic martini glasses
Jack Daniel's Tennessee Whiskey
Triple sec
Sweet and sour mix
Lemon-lime soda

ALSO BUY, IF NOT IN YOUR PANTRY
Sugar
Vegetable oil
Apple cider vinegar
Dry mustard
Celery seed
Salt
Black pepper
Red wine vinegar
Olive oil
Dijon mustard

Tailgating

Tailgating

For many, going to the game is not about the game itself, but really about the party at the game. It is the Great American Tailgate, a party to raise spirit with your friends for your favorite team. Actually, you do not have to go to the game to have a tailgate party, you can tailgate right at home as you get ready to watch your team compete on television or listen in on the radio.

Tailgating has come a long way. Equipment used to be primitive and menus were simple in the early years. Today's tailgaters have comfortable chairs under the shade of pop-up tents. They can watch television, thanks to portable satellite dishes, and run other helpful amenities such as plug-in coolers and heaters from the outlets in their vehicles and generators. All this new technology has freed up tailgaters to spend more time on creative menus and party planning. Some tailgaters have turned their party into a competitive sport, as they try to out-do each other in decorations, menu and style.

TIPS FOR TAILGATING
- Organize your food and beverage offerings and keep things simple. Plan entrées your guests can assemble and eat with a minimum of utensils and mess.
- Make a written checklist of items to pack. Do not forget important items such as trash bags, sunscreen, paper napkins, plastic cups and paper towels.
- Weather can be a problem. Check the weather report in advance, and be prepared for the worst. Bring pop-up tents and lightweight tarps to cover serving tables in the event of a rain shower.
- Pack non-perishable items in your vehicle ahead of time and leave room for last-minute coolers.
- Consider easy grill items such as cedar plank salmon (see Brunch) and grilled pizzas (see Pizza Party).
- Pack and make as many items as possible in disposable containers so you do not have to bring dirty dishes home.

- Prepare food ahead of time. When you get to the tailgate site, you do not want to spend time chopping vegetables. Save this time for assembly.
- Pack plenty of alcohol-free sodas, juices and waters.
- Bring games such as cornhole, along with frisbees and footballs.
- Plan to arrive at the stadium three hours before the game to allow plenty of time to tailgate and clean up.
- This is a social occasion, so be sure to meet your tailgating neighbors and share ideas once you arrive.

ACCORDING TO A SURVEY CONDUCTED BY TAILGATING.COM

- 60 percent are between the ages of 25 and 44.
- 79 percent are men.
- 58 percent have a college degree and 14 percent have completed a graduate program.
- 44 percent said that they shop for tailgating food and supplies with their spouse.
- 41 percent spend more than $500 a season on tailgating food and supplies.
- 95 percent cook their food at the tailgate, with only 5 percent preferring to bring fast or prepared food.
- 59 percent use a combination of grills, stoves and smokers to cook their food, while 39 percent prefer just a grill.
- 47 percent tailgate 6 – 10 times per year; 27 percent tailgate 2 – 5 times per year; 15 percent tailgate 11 – 15 times per year and 7 percent tailgate just once a year.
- 50 percent get to the tailgate 3 – 4 hours before the event starts; 28 percent arrive 5 – 6 hours before; 15 percent arrive more than 7 hours prior; 7 percent get there 1 – 2 hours beforehand.

Blue Blast and Red Rocket

BLUE BLAST

8 ounces Finlandia vodka

16 ounces Blue Curacao

24 ounces white cranberry juice

Mix all ingredients in a pitcher. Serve over ice.

Serves 8

RED ROCKET

12 ounces Finlandia tangerine vodka

24 ounces lemonade

12 ounces cranberry juice

Mix all ingredients in a pitcher. Serve over ice.

Serves 8

NOTE: THE COLORS OF EACH OF THESE DRINKS CAN BE ENHANCED WITH FOOD COLORING TO MATCH YOUR TEAM'S COLORS.

Vegetable Platter

Asparagus	Red peppers
Mini carrots	Yellow peppers
Sugar snap peas	Orange peppers

We like to quickly blanch our asparagus, carrots and sugar snap peas before serving. Drop each into a pot of boiling water for 2 – 3 minutes, then plunge them into a bowl of ice water to stop the cooking and to bring out their bright color. Once cold, pat them dry and refrigerate until serving. Pack in zip-top plastic bags to transport to your tailgating site.

The peppers can simply be cut into strips and served raw. Be sure to scrape out the seeds and white membrane inside. A grapefruit spoon, melon baller or teaspoon works best for this job.

Whole peppers can be used as serving bowls for dips and to stand up your other vegetables for a festive presentation. To do this, cut the top off the pepper and a small slice off the bottom so it will stand level. Again, scrape out the seeds and white membrane using a grapefruit spoon, melon baller or teaspoon. Refrigerate until ready to serve. Spoon your dips or stand your vegetables inside your pepper bowls and arrange them on your platter.

Dill Dip

1 cup sour cream	1 tablespoon fresh parsley, chopped
½ cup ricotta cheese, part skim milk	1 tablespoon fresh lemon juice
1 tablespoon fresh dill, chopped	1 tablespoon sweet onion, minced

In a small bowl, combine the sour cream, ricotta cheese, dill, parsley, lemon juice and sweet onion. Refrigerate for several hours. Serve with potato chips or fresh vegetables.

Makes 1½ cups

NOTE: AS A HEALTHIER ALTERNATIVE, SUBSTITUTE PLAIN YOGURT (GREEK-STYLE) FOR THE SOUR CREAM.

Hummus in Cucumber Cups

1 English cucumber	1 teaspoon cumin
1 15-ounce can garbanzo beans (chickpeas), drained	1 clove garlic, crushed
¼ cup olive oil	Pinch of salt
1 tablespoon fresh lemon juice	Paprika

TO MAKE THE CUCUMBER CUPS

Wash and dry the cucumber. With a vegetable peeler, "stripe" the cucumber by peeling a ½-inch strip from top to bottom. Rotate the cucumber, leaving ½-inch of the original peel, then peel another ½-inch strip until you have "striped" the whole cucumber. Cut it into ½-inch rounds. With a melon baller or small spoon, scoop out a little of the center of the round, trying not to hit the bottom, making a small cup.

TO MAKE THE HUMMUS

In a food processor, add the garbanzo beans, olive oil, lemon juice, cumin, garlic and salt. Process until smooth. Taste and adjust salt, if necessary. Refrigerate until ready to serve.

Fill the cucumber cups with a spoonful of the hummus. Sprinkle with paprika.

Serves 8 – 10

NOTE: TO MAKE ROASTED RED PEPPER HUMMUS, ADD ½ CUP OF JARRED ROASTED RED PEPPERS THAT HAVE BEEN DRAINED AND SEEDED.

Buffalo Chicken Dip

2 8-ounce packages of cream cheese	2 cups sharp cheddar cheese, shredded
1 8-ounce container of blue cheese dressing	Fritos Scoops
1 12-ounce bottle of Frank's Red Hot Sauce	Triscuits
2 cups cooked chicken breast, shredded	Celery sticks

Preheat oven to 350 degrees.

In a bowl, mix cream cheese, blue cheese, hot sauce and shredded chicken breast. Spread in the bottom of a 9 x 9-inch pan and sprinkle with cheddar cheese. Bake for 30 minutes. Serve warm with Fritos Scoops, Triscuits and celery sticks.

Serves 8 – 10

NOTE: THIS DIP IS MEDIUM HOT. FOR MORE OR LESS HEAT, ADJUST THE HOT SAUCE. THIS CAN BE BAKED IN A DISPOSABLE FOIL PAN FOR EASY TRANSPORT TO YOUR TAILGATING SITE.

Beef and Chicken Fajitas

2 pounds flank steak, fat-trimmed	Fajita seasoning
4 boneless chicken breasts	1 lime, cut into wedges
2 cups Italian salad dressing, divided	2 zip-top plastic bags, 1-gallon
4 tablespoons cilantro leaves, roughly chopped, divided	32 large flour tortillas

ACCOMPANIMENTS
Salsa
Cheddar or Pepper Jack cheese, shredded
Sour cream
Guacamole
Jalapeño peppers
Shredded lettuce

In one of the plastic bags, add the steak, 1 cup of the Italian salad dressing and 2 tablespoons of the cilantro. Seal the bag, place in a baking dish and refrigerate for at least 4 hours and up to 24 hours, turning occasionally.

In the other plastic bag, add the chicken, remaining Italian salad dressing and cilantro. Seal the bag, place in a baking dish and refrigerate for at least 4 hours and up to 24 hours, turning occasionally.

Remove the steak and chicken from their bags and pat dry. Season the steak and chicken on both sides with a few shakes of the fajita seasoning.

Preheat the grill to medium-high or the oven to 325 degrees.

Wrap the tortillas in foil and place in the oven or on the grill for 15 minutes to warm and soften. Remove and keep warm in the foil.

Grill the steak to your preferred temperature, 3 – 4 minutes per side for medium rare. Remove from the heat and let rest for 10 minutes before slicing thinly, against the grain. Grill the chicken for 5 – 8 minutes per side or until cooked through. Remove from the heat and let rest for 10 minutes before slicing into thin strips. Toss the steak strips with a couple squeezes of lime and do the same for the chicken strips.

Serve with the warm tortillas and accompaniments so your guests can build their own to their liking.

Serves 12 – 16

NOTE: THE MEAT CAN BE COOKED AT HOME OR AT YOUR TAILGATING SITE. JUST WRAP IN FOIL TO TRANSPORT.

Pumpkin Coconut Oatmeal Bars

CRUST

½ cup (1 stick) unsalted butter, melted	1 cup quick cooking oats
½ cup brown sugar	1 teaspoon cinnamon
1 cup all-purpose flour	¼ teaspoon salt

FILLING

4 eggs, beaten	¼ cup cornstarch
1 cup sugar	1 teaspoon cinnamon
1 cup brown sugar	1 teaspoon nutmeg
1 15-ounce can of pumpkin	1 cup shredded coconut

FOR THE CRUST

Preheat the oven to 350 degrees. In a mixing bowl, combine the butter, brown sugar, flour, oats, cinnamon and salt. Press into the bottom of greased 8 x 8-inch pan. Poke the crust with a fork to keep it from cracking. Bake for 10 minutes.

FOR THE FILLING

In a mixing bowl, combine the eggs, sugar, brown sugar, pumpkin, cornstarch, cinnamon, nutmeg and coconut. Pour over the warm crust. Return to oven for 45 minutes or until toothpick placed in the center comes out clean. Cut into bite-sized bars or into rounds. Top with an optional dollop of vanilla frosting.

Serves 8 – 12

NOTE: THIS CAN BE BAKED IN A DISPOSABLE FOIL PAN FOR EASY TRANSPORT TO YOUR TAILGATING SITE.

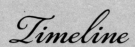
Timeline

1 WEEK AHEAD
- Shop for non-perishable groceries
- Shop for tailgating equipment (pop-up tent, table, tarps, portable TV)

2 DAYS AHEAD
- Shop for last-minute groceries
- Make a list of items to bring and organize items you will need to pack (utensils, garbage bags, sunscreen, rain gear).

1 DAY AHEAD
- Make pitchers of the Blue Blast
- Make pitchers of the Red Rocket
- Make the Pumpkin Coconut Oatmeal Bars (refrigerate in the pan; do not cut)
- Make the Hummus for the Hummus in Cucumber Cups
- Make the Buffalo Chicken Dip
- Blanch the vegetables for the Vegetable Platter
- Marinate the flank steak and chicken for the Fajitas

MORNING OF THE TAILGATE
- Make the Dill Dip
- Put the accompaniments for the Fajitas in serving bowls

1 HOUR AHEAD
- Preheat the grill or oven to 350 degrees
- Arrange the Fritos and Triscuits on platters
- Plate the Hummus in the Cucumber Cups
- Cut the Coconut Oatmeal Bars and arrange on a serving platter
- Plate any other bars, cookies or desserts you may have purchased

30 MINUTES BEFORE THE TAILGATE
- Put the Buffalo Chicken Dip on the grill or in the oven
- Grill the beef and chicken
- Arrange the Fresh Vegetables on a platter with Dill Dip

JUST BEFORE THE TAILGATE
- Plate the Buffalo Chicken Dip
- Put the tortillas on the grill or in the oven to warm
- Set out the fajita accompaniments
- Set out all other food items
- Check bar; put ice in bucket; set out pitcher drinks, sodas and water

Shopping List

Sour cream or Greek-style
   plain yogurt
Ricotta cheese, part skim milk
Fresh dill, 1 bunch
Fresh parsley, 1 bunch
Lemons, 2
Sweet onion, 1
Salsa, 1 large jar
Fresh cilantro, 1 bunch
Asparagus, 1 bunch
Mini carrots, 1 bag
Sugar snap peas, 1 bag
Red peppers, 2
Yellow peppers, 2
Orange peppers, 2
Cream cheese, 2,
   8-ounce packages
Blue cheese dressing,
   1 8-ounce container
Frank's Red Hot Sauce,
   1 12-ounce bottle
Chicken breast,
   cooked, 2 cups
Sharp cheddar cheese,
   shredded, 2 cups
Fritos Scoops
Triscuits
Celery, 1 bunch
English cucumber, 1
Garbanzo beans
   (chickpeas),
   1 15-ounce can
Garlic, 1 bulb
Flank steak, fat trimmed,
   2 pounds
Boneless chicken breasts, 4
Italian salad dressing
Fajita seasoning
Lime, 1
Large flour tortillas, 32
Cheddar or Pepper Jack
   cheese, shredded
Guacamole
Jalapeño peppers, 1 jar
Lettuce, shredded
Quick cooking oats
Pumpkin, 1 15-ounce can
Shredded coconut,
   small bag

Finlandia vodka
Finlandia tangerine vodka
Blue Curacao
White cranberry juice
Lemonade
Cranberry juice

**ALSO BUY, IF NOT
IN YOUR PANTRY**
Olive oil
Ground cumin
Kosher salt
Black Pepper
Paprika
Zip-top plastic bags,
   1-gallon
Eggs
Sugar
Brown sugar
Cornstarch
Cinnamon
Nutmeg
Unsalted butter
flour

Wine & Cheese Party

When you say, "wine," I say "cheese." A great entertaining idea is to gather friends and neighbors together for a wine and cheese party. It is an experiential occasion that gets everyone involved. When wine is correctly paired with food, the wine makes the food taste better and food makes the wine taste better. Here are a few tips to ensure your party will be a success. Cheers!

TIPS ON HOSTING A WINE AND CHEESE PARTY

- Offer a wide selection of white and red wines so your guests can experiment with many flavors.
- Set out the cheeses at least two hours ahead, so they have time to come to room temperature and exhibit their full flavor.
- Plate the cheeses with their own serving knives and leave enough space between the cheeses so the flavors do not blend.
- Use cheese markers so your guests know the type of cheese they are tasting.
- Select glasses that can multi-task for both white and red wines. These would be standard wine glasses or larger white wine glasses.
- Have wine charms on the glasses so your guests do not lose track of their glasses.
- Set out a pitcher of water and a dump bucket so your guests can rinse their glasses after each wine they try.
- When tasting, you will want to pour just enough wine in the glass to have about two or three sips to taste with a couple bites of cheese. This way, each guest can try several combinations.
- Plan on approximately 12 – 15 tasting pours per bottle of wine.
- Arrange the wines and cheeses from light to heavy. Start with the white wines and then move on to the reds.
- Set out a variety of crackers and light bites to help cleanse the palate after each tasting.
- Plate an assortment of fresh fruit to complement the cheeses, such as seedless grapes, apples and pears.

- Nuts, especially walnuts, cashews and almonds also pair well with wines.
- Encourage your guests to talk about their wine and cheese experience after each sip and taste.
- Poll the most popular pairings and have your guests keep a record of their favorites.
- The pairings on the next few pages demonstrate some awesome examples to help you experience the sensation of how a perfect marriage of flavors can enhance the tastes of both the wines and the cheeses. Be brave, experiment and have fun pairing wines and cheeses on your own.

MUST TRY PAIRING GUIDE

Sauvignon blanc with goat cheese: Both of these items are slightly acidic and have a strong taste. When you try them together, the wine tastes creamier and the cheese tastes milder.

Chardonnay with fontina cheese: The cheese can be pungent with an intense flavor. This pairing makes both the wine and cheese taste creamy and lush.

Cabernet sauvignon with blue cheese: Both the wine and the cheese have big bold flavors. Sampled together, the wine tames the blue cheese and the cheese makes the wine taste velvety smooth. The fat content of the cheese mellows the tannins in the wine and the wine makes the blue cheese soft and creamy.

For a sweet treat, try a couple of bites of dark bittersweet chocolate with the cabernet. It is truly a wonderful marriage! For a festive dessert, rim a red wine glass in melted chocolate, let set and when it is dessert time, fill it with cabernet.

OTHER PAIRING IDEAS

Cheese	Wine Ideas
Blue	Cabernet Sauvignon, Shiraz or Zinfandel
Brie	Chardonnay or Pinot Noir
Cheddar	Riesling, Sauvignon Blanc, Merlot or Shiraz
Gouda	Riesling, Merlot or Zinfandel
Gruyere	Chardonnay, Riesling, Sauvignon Blanc or Shiraz
Monterey Jack	Riesling, Sauvignon Blanc or Merlot
Parmigiano-Reggiano	Chardonnay, Sauvignon Blanc, Cabernet Sauvignon or Merlot
Swiss	Sauvignon Blanc, Cabernet Sauvignon or Pinot Noir

STORING CHEESE

- Keep the cheese wrapped so it does not dry out when storing. Unwrap it just before serving. Wrap and refrigerate any leftover cheese as soon as possible.
- Plastic wrap is acceptable for wrapping cheese. To allow the cheese to breathe and keep it from discoloring, the wrap should be changed every few days.
- Different types of cheeses require different methods of storage:
    - Hard cheeses with little moisture (parmesan) should be wrapped tightly in plastic wrap to avoid further moisture loss.
    - Semi-hard cheeses (cheddar, Jack, Swiss) can be wrapped in either plastic wrap, wax paper or parchment paper.
    - Semi-soft cheese (Brie, blue) should be wrapped in wax paper or parchment paper, or may be kept in a plastic container.
    - Soft or fresh cheeses (ricotta, feta) should be kept in a plastic container.

Steakhouse at Home

Steakhouse at Home

It is always a special treat to go to a traditional steakhouse and have a fantastic cut of beef with lobster tail and oversized side dishes. Traditional sides include big tomato slices with blue cheese crumbles, creamed spinach, sautéed mushrooms with port wine and hash brown potatoes, crispy on the outside and soft on the inside. For starters, a "must" cocktail is the traditional Manhattan, and a big red wine with dinner. Dessert requires something decadent and chocolate – enter Chocolate Decadence Cake with Raspberry Sauce.

The only downside to the traditional steakhouse dinner is the sticker shock. It is easy to hit three digits on a check with only two diners. With a little work, you can create this experience at home. You can save money without sacrificing any flavors, and it will be well worth the effort. There are also a few secrets which will be revealed to make your meal just like ones they serve at the famous steakhouses.

As both bourbon and red wine go well with steak, I developed a cocktail which includes both – the Woodford Ruby. It is very tasty and a fabulous accompaniment to the meal.

In deciding which cut of beef to prepare, the t-bone or porterhouse was the obvious answer. It has both the New York strip and the tenderloin, which makes it easy to share. By cooking one large cut, you can serve two or more.

Grab your big steak knives and plates and get ready to prepare and enjoy a traditional steakhouse dinner at home.

Traditional Manhattan

In a shaker with ice, add:

3 ounces bourbon or whiskey

½ ounce sweet vermouth

4 dashes of bitters

Shake and strain into chilled martini glasses. Garnish with maraschino cherries.

Serves 2

Woodford Ruby

In a shaker with ice, add:

3 ounces Woodford Reserve bourbon

6 ounces red wine such as merlot

2 ounces simple syrup

2 teaspoons lemon juice

Shake and strain into chilled martini glasses. Garnish with lemon twists.

Serves 2

Sliced Tomato Salad

1 or 2 large beefsteak tomatoes, cut into 4 thick slices	2 ounces blue cheese, crumbled
Extra virgin olive oil	Kosher salt
2 tablespoons red onion, diced	Fresh ground black pepper
	Basil sprig for garnish

Place the sliced tomatoes on your serving plate. Drizzle with olive oil. Sprinkle with the red onion and blue cheese, season with salt and pepper. Garnish with sprig of basil.

Serves 2 – 4

NOTE: YOU CAN ALSO DRIZZLE AGED OR REDUCED BALSAMIC VINEGAR OVER THE TOP TO ADD ANOTHER LAYER OF FLAVOR.

Creamed Spinach

1 12-ounce bag frozen chopped spinach, thawed	½ cup heavy cream
1 tablespoon olive oil	½ teaspoon salt
1 tablespoon butter	½ teaspoon pepper
1½ teaspoons garlic, crushed	¼ teaspoon nutmeg
¼ cup shallots, chopped	French-fried onions for garnish

Make sure the spinach is drained of all water by either wringing in a kitchen towel or pressing it in a fine sieve.

In a medium sauté pan, heat the olive oil and butter over medium-high heat. Add the garlic and shallots and cook until soft, about 2 minutes. Add the spinach and cook for an additional 2 minutes. Add the cream, salt, pepper and nutmeg and cook until reduced by half, about 5 minutes. Place in serving dish and garnish with toasted French-fried onions. Serve immediately.

Serves 4 – 6

Steamed Broccoli

2 – 3 large broccoli crowns, cleaned
Kosher salt

Fresh ground black pepper
Lemon wedge

Fill a pot fitted with a steamer basket with water, just to the bottom of the basket. Bring to a boil, add the broccoli, cover and steam for 5 – 7 minutes until desired doneness. Season with salt and pepper and a squeeze of lemon.

Serves 2 – 4

NOTE: YOU CAN STEAM BROCCOLI IN THE MICROWAVE BY PLACING IT IN A MICROWAVE-SAFE DISH WITH 1 TABLESPOON OF WATER. COVER AND COOK FOR 3 – 5 MINUTES UNTIL DESIRED DONENESS. SEASON WITH SALT AND PEPPER AND A SQUEEZE OF LEMON.

Sautéed Mushrooms

1 tablespoon butter	Kosher salt
1 tablespoon olive oil	Fresh ground black pepper
8 ounces sliced mushrooms	Flat-leaf parsley, finely chopped
½ cup port wine	

In a sauté pan, heat the butter and olive oil over medium heat. Add the mushrooms in a single layer and let cook without stirring for 5 minutes. Raise the heat to medium-high. Remove the pan from the heat and add the port wine. Return the pan to the heat and cook until the liquid has been absorbed, about 3 – 5 minutes. Season to taste with salt and pepper. Garnish with fresh parsley.

Serves 2 – 4

Hash Browns

1½ pounds Idaho potatoes	Kosher salt
(about 2 large potatoes)	Fresh ground black pepper
1 egg white	Peanut or vegetable oil

Preheat oven to 425 degrees.

Wash and peel potatoes. Use a food processor with the medium shredding attachment to shred the potatoes, or use a box grater. Place the potato shreds in a kitchen towel and wring out all of the water until very dry. This is a must for crispy browns.

In a 9-inch oven-proof frying pan, heat 1 tablespoon of the oil over medium-high heat. In a large mixing bowl, toss the potato shreds with the egg white and season with ½ teaspoon of salt and pepper. Spoon mixture into the hot pan, packing it in, and pressing down to compress the mixture. Drizzle the top with more oil and season with a little more salt and pepper. When it starts to brown on the bottom and gets crispy around the edges, flip the hash browns over onto a plate, then slide back into the pan to brown on the other side. Put the pan with the hash browns in the oven and bake for 15 minutes. Remove from oven and allow to cool slightly before sliding onto your serving platter. Garnish with more pepper and serve.

Serves 2 – 4

Lobster Tail

1 10-ounce lobster tail, thawed	Butter pats
1 lemon, cut into wedges	Paprika

Preheat oven to 350 degrees.

Thaw lobster tail in the refrigerator overnight. Rinse under cold water and cut the top of the shell down the center to the tail, using a knife or kitchen shears. Pull the meat out and rest it on the top of the shell, leaving the tip of the tail still connected to the fins. Make a small slit down the center of the meat and insert 3 pats of butter. Place in a baking dish and bake for 15 minutes. Remove from the oven. Squeeze a couple of lemon wedges over the meat, sprinkle with paprika and broil for 5 minutes until golden. For presentation, leave the cooked meat on top of the tail. To eat, remove the shell. Serve with additional lemon wedges and melted butter for dipping.

Serves 2

T-Bone Steak and Spice Rub

1 26-ounce t-bone steak	2 teaspoons Spice Rub (recipe below)
2 teaspoons vegetable oil	Fresh ground black pepper

Preheat oven to 400 degrees.

Brush both sides of the steak with oil and sprinkle each side with 1 teaspoon of the Spice Rub and pepper.

In an oven-proof frying pan, heat 1 teaspoon oil over high heat. Sear one side of the steak in the pan for 2 minutes, flip to sear the other side for 2 minutes. Place the pan with the steak in it in the oven and cook for 5 minutes or until a meat thermometer registers 125 degrees. It will rise at least another 10 degrees to 135 for medium rare. Let it rest for 5 minutes, then serve.

Serves 2 – 4

Spice Rub

4 tablespoons paprika	2 tablespoons onion powder
3 tablespoons garlic powder	1 tablespoon dried oregano
3 tablespoons Kosher salt	1 teaspoon cayenne pepper
2 tablespoons black pepper	

Combine all ingredients in a small bowl and pour into a spice shaker. Mixture will keep for 6 months.

Chocolate Decadence with Raspberries

6 whole eggs	10 tablespoons (1¼ sticks) unsalted butter
3 egg yolks	1 pint fresh raspberries for garnish
1 tablespoon sugar	Raspberry Sauce for garnish
1 tablespoon flour	Powdered sugar for garnish
16 ounces bittersweet chocolate	

Preheat oven to 350 degrees.

In a mixing bowl, blend the whole eggs, egg yolks, sugar and flour until smooth and thick. Set aside. In the top of a double boiler, melt the chocolate with the butter. Slowly add the egg mixture to the chocolate mixture until incorporated.

Pour into a greased 8-inch round springform pan. Smooth the top and bake for 15 – 17 minutes. It will seem undercooked, but will set as it cools. Place one piece on a plate, drizzle desired amount of Raspberry Sauce and sprinkle with powdered sugar. Garnish with fresh raspberries.

Serves 6 – 8

Raspberry Sauce

1 12-ounce package frozen raspberries, thawed	2 tablespoons Chambord liqueur
⅓ cup sugar	

In a food processor or blender, purée the raspberries with the sugar and Chambord. Pour through a fine mesh sieve to remove the seeds. Pour into a small pitcher for serving. Can be made 1 day in advance.

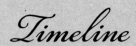

Timeline

1 WEEK AHEAD
- Shop for non-perishable groceries
- Make the Spice Rub
- Order your cut of beef if it is not normally carried by your butcher

2 DAYS AHEAD
- Prepare your table with platters and serving pieces

1 DAY AHEAD
- Shop for last-minute groceries
- Put the frozen spinach in the refrigerator to thaw for the Creamed Spinach
- Put the frozen lobster tail in the refrigerator to thaw
- Make the Raspberry Sauce for the Chocolate Decadence

MORNING OF THE PARTY
- Crumble the blue cheese and dice the red onion for the Sliced Tomato Salad
- Chop the parsley for garnish; refrigerate
- Make the Chocolate Decadence; store at room temperature until ready to serve dessert

2 HOURS AHEAD
- Toast the French-fried onions for the Creamed Spinach

1 HOUR AHEAD
- Make the Creamed Spinach; keep warm
- Make the Hash Browns; keep warm
- Prepare the Lobster Tail; refrigerate until ready to cook

JUST BEFORE THE PARTY
- Finish making and plate the Sliced Tomato Salad
- Chill your martini glasses by filling them with ice and water
- Check bar; fill ice buckets; set out garnishes

JUST BEFORE SERVING DINNER
- Make the Steamed Broccoli
- Make the Sautéed Mushrooms
- Cook the Lobster Tail
- Season and cook the T-Bone Steak

Shopping List

Beefsteak tomatoes, 1–2
Red onion, 1
Blue cheese, 2 ounces, crumbled
Basil, 1 bunch
Large broccoli crowns, 2–3
Lemon, 1
Sliced mushrooms, 8 ounces
Port wine
Flat-leaf parsley, 1 bunch
Frozen chopped spinach,
   1 12-ounce bag
Garlic, 1 bulb
Shallot, 1
Heavy cream, ½ pint
French fried onions
Idaho potatoes, 1½ pounds,
   about 2 large potatoes
Lobster tail, 10-ounce
T-bone steak, 26-ounce
Bittersweet chocolate,
   16 ounces
Eggs, 1 dozen
Fresh raspberries, 1 pint
Frozen raspberries,
   1 12-ounce package
Chambord liqueur
Woodford Reserve bourbon
Red wine, such as merlot
Bourbon or whiskey
Sweet vermouth
Bitters
Maraschino cherries

ALSO BUY, IF NOT IN YOUR PANTRY

Kosher salt
Black pepper
Unsalted butter
Extra virgin olive oil
Paprika
Nutmeg
Peanut or vegetable oil
Cayenne pepper
Garlic powder
Onion powder
Dried oregano
Powdered sugar
Sugar
Flour

Thanksgiving

Thanksgiving symbolizes deeply-felt traditions and the time for family and friends to gather together to share great food and give thanks. Too bad we cannot turn this into a more-than-one-a-year event, as we all have so much for which to be thankful. However, since it is a widely celebrated holiday on the third Thursday of November, let's embrace it with warmth and fun.

Although it is a North American holiday (with Canadian Thanksgiving in October), the idea of family tradition lends itself nicely to including family recipes from around the globe. Every family has its cherished Thanksgiving traditions, along with favorite recipes passed down through generations.

To honor the memory of family members, some of whom are no longer with us, we have re-created their recipes for our Thanksgiving dinner. We had to pry the "secret" recipes from our family members so we could include their most memorable dishes. Here we share with you our Thanksgiving delights in one special dinner.

TIPS FOR YOUR THANKSGIVING DINNER
- Plan your meal well in advance and make sure all of your guests' special dietary needs (if any) are considered.
- Make a checklist of shopping items by date and store.
- Create a timeline of activities with a checklist to post on your refrigerator and check off tasks as they are accomplished.
- Prepare as many items as possible ahead of time.
- The kitchen will be a busy area and counter space and ovens will be at a premium. Consider cooking certain items on the grill to help lighten the load inside and to cut down on traffic.
- Do not be afraid to recruit friends and family members to help with last-minute assembly, serving and clean up.
- Have fun! Remember you are celebrating generations of memories and creating new ones for generations to come. Memories are our special treasures that stay with us forever and cannot be stolen from us or devalued. They become the gifts for which we should give thanks, not only on Thanksgiving Day, but all year long.

Mayflower Martini

3 ounces Old Forester bourbon	Squeeze of lemon
6 ounces apple cider	Dash of cinnamon
1 clove	Red apple slices, for garnish

Add all ingredients to a shaker with ice. Shake and strain into martini glasses. Garnish with slices of apple.

Serves 2

Jack's Maple Nut Cocktail

3 ounces Jack Daniel's Tennessee Whiskey	1 ounce maple syrup
1 ounce Dumante pistachio nut liqueur	Lemon wedges, for garnish

Add all ingredients to a shaker with ice. Shake and strain into rocks glasses with ice. Garnish with lemon wedges.

Serves 2

Mom's Oyster Stew

1 cup (2 sticks) unsalted butter	Dash of hot sauce
1 teaspoon celery seed	8 cups (½ gallon) whole milk –
¼ teaspoon Worcestershire sauce	room temperature
2 quarts + 1 pint raw oysters, undrained	4 cups (1 quart) half & half –
1 teaspoon salt	room temperature
½ teaspoon paprika	Oyster crackers

In a large saucepan, melt the butter over medium-high heat. Add the celery seed and Worcestershire sauce, then add the oysters and oyster liquor. Cook until the oysters begin to curl around the edges. Lower the heat and slowly add the milk and half & half to avoid curdling. Add the salt, paprika and hot sauce. Raise the heat slowly to medium and cook until heated through. Be sure never to let the stew boil. Serve in warm bowls with warm oyster crackers.

Serves 8 – 10

NOTE: THE JUICE OYSTERS ARE STORED IN IS CALLED THEIR LIQUOR OR OYSTER LIQUOR.

Corn Pudding

3 tablespoons butter, melted	4 eggs, lightly beaten
1 tablespoon flour	1 cup milk
1 15-ounce can of creamed corn	Salt
⅓ cup sugar	Pepper

Preheat oven to 350 degrees.

Pour the melted butter into a medium-size bowl. Add the flour and stir until smooth. Add the creamed corn, sugar, eggs, milk and a pinch of salt and pepper. Stir until combined. Pour into a pie plate and carefully place the pie plate in a pan of water. Bake for 45 minutes to 1 hour or until set.

Serves 8 – 10

Zelnik (Spinach Pie)

4 eggs	1½ teaspoon salt
2 tablespoons vegetable oil	1 teaspoon pepper
1 cup plain yogurt (preferably Greek-style)	12 sheets phyllo dough (extra is included in case it tears and you have to use more)
1 teaspoon baking soda	
¾ cup flour	½ cup (1 stick) unsalted butter, melted
11 ounces feta cheese, crumbled (preferably Bulgarian feta)	
8 ounces frozen spinach, thawed and drained of all water	

Preheat oven to 350 degrees.

Thaw the phyllo dough according to the directions on the package. Grease a 10-inch pie plate. In a medium-size bowl, mix the eggs with the vegetable oil. Add the yogurt, baking soda and flour. Mix in the feta cheese, spinach, salt and pepper. On a dry surface, carefully spread out one sheet of phyllo dough. Using a pastry brush, paint it with the melted butter. Add a second sheet on top, then 1 heaping cup of the cheese mixture, spreading it the length of the dough. Roll this into a long tube and carefully place it into the pie plate around the edge. Repeat the process with the sheets of phyllo dough until all of the cheese mixture is used and the pie plate is full. This should be 4 rolls, using 8 sheets of phyllo dough. Brush the top of the Zelnik with the remaining melted butter. Bake for 1 hour until golden. Serve warm or at room temperature.

Serves 8 – 10

NOTE: GREEK-STYLE YOGURT HAS A TART FLAVOR AND THICKER CONSISTENCY THAN REGULAR YOGURT. BULGARIAN FETA CAN BE FOUND AT MOST INTERNATIONAL FOOD STORES. PHYLLO DOUGH CAN BE FOUND IN THE FROZEN DESSERT AREA OF MOST GROCERY STORES AND INTERNATIONAL FOOD STORES.

Laird Cranberry Salad

1 12-ounce bag cranberries, frozen
½ cup sugar
2 cups (1 pint) heavy whipping cream
1 10.5-ounce bag mini marshmallows

1 8-ounce can crushed pineapple, drained
1 cup slivered almonds, toasted

In a food processor, grind the frozen cranberries to a fine consistency. In a medium-size bowl, combine the sugar and cranberries. Cover and refrigerate for a minimum of 4 hours. Overnight is best.

Whip the whipping cream until stiff peaks form. In a large bowl, combine the whipped cream with the marshmallows. Cover and refrigerate for a minimum of 4 hours. Overnight is best.

2 hours before serving: Fold the cranberries into the marshmallow mixture. Add the pineapple and half of the almonds. Sprinkle the rest of the almonds on top of the salad just before serving.

Serves 8 – 10

Roast Turkey

24 HOURS BEFORE COOKING THE TURKEY

⅓ cup Kosher salt	2 teaspoons black pepper
2 teaspoons dried rosemary	4 small bay leaves, torn
2 teaspoons dried rubbed sage	2 teaspoons finely-grated lemon peel
2 teaspoons dried thyme	1 oven roasting bag
2 teaspoons dried parsley	1 14-16-pound turkey

Make a salt rub by combining the salt, rosemary, sage, thyme, parsley, black pepper, bay leaves and grated lemon in a small bowl.

Rinse the turkey inside and out and pat dry. Place the turkey inside the roasting bag and rub it liberally with the salt mixture, being sure to get it inside both cavities. Seal the bag, and refrigerate it for 16 – 24 hours.

Remove the turkey from the bag and rinse off all of the salt, inside and out. Pat dry.

COOKING THE TURKEY

½ cup (1 stick) unsalted butter, room temperature	2 Granny Smith apples, seeded and roughly chopped
6 large carrots, peeled and roughly chopped into 1-inch pieces	2 oranges, roughly chopped
	Paprika
6 celery stalks, roughly chopped into 1-inch pieces	Salt
	Pepper
3 onions, roughly chopped into 1-inch sections	Roasting pan

Preheat oven to 325 degrees with the rack on the lowest position. Place the carrots, celery and onions in the bottom of the roasting pan to create a bed for the turkey to rest. To add flavor, fill both cavities with the apples and oranges. Rub the outside of the turkey with the butter and sprinkle with paprika, salt and pepper. Roast in the oven for approximately 20 minutes per pound or until the temperature reaches 165 degrees in the thickest part of the thigh. Remove from the oven, tent with foil and let rest for 20 minutes while you make the gravy.

NOTE: IF YOU USE SMOKED PAPRIKA, IT WILL GIVE YOUR BIRD A SMOKY FLAVOR.

GRAVY

3 tablespoons pan drippings (or butter)	Salt
5 tablespoons flour	Pepper
3½ cups turkey or chicken stock or broth	

In a small saucepan over medium heat, mix the drippings or butter with the flour, whisking together to form a roux. Slowly add the stock or broth, whisking continually to avoid lumps until incorporated. Continue to cook for 10 minutes, whisking occasionally. Season with salt and pepper.

Serves 8 – 10

NOTE: PLAN ON 1 POUND OF TURKEY PER PERSON (A LITTLE MORE WITH LEFTOVERS) AND ⅓ CUP OF GRAVY PER PERSON. WE OFTEN BUY THE JARRED GRAVY FROM THE GROCERY STORE. IT SAVES TIME NOT HAVING TO MAKE IT AND YOU DO NOT HAVE TO WORRY ABOUT LUMPS. PLUS, IT IS LOWER IN FAT AND CALORIES THAN HOMEMADE AND TASTES GREAT.

Cranberry Sauce

½ cup sugar	1 12-ounce bag cranberries
½ cup Chambord liqueur	1 orange, zested
½ cup water	

In a medium sauce pan, add the sugar, Chambord and water. Bring to a boil over medium-high heat. Once the sugar is dissolved, add the cranberries and orange zest and return to a boil. Turn the heat down and continue to cook, stirring occasionally, until the berries pop and the sauce thickens, about 10 minutes. Remove from the heat to cool. Store in the refrigerator until ready to serve.

Serves 8 – 10

Lamb Chops

25 French-cut lamb chops	Black pepper
½ cup olive oil	1 lemon
½ cup Greek seasoning	

Preheat grill to high heat.

Trim any excess fat from the lamb chops. Brush both sides of the chops with olive oil and sprinkle with Greek seasoning and black pepper. Place on the hot grill and cook for about 2 – 3 minutes per side for medium rare. After cooked to desired temperature, squeeze lemon juice over them and serve with Tarator (yogurt sauce).

Serves 8 – 10

Tarator

4 cups Greek-style yogurt	1 teaspoon dried dill
1 medium English cucumber, coarsely grated	Salt
4 cloves garlic, crushed	Pepper

Place a piece of cheesecloth in a strainer or colander and pour in the yogurt. In a separate strainer or colander, place a piece of cheesecloth and the grated cucumber. Let both drain for 2 hours. In a medium bowl, combine the yogurt, cucumber, garlic and dill. Add salt and pepper to taste.

Serves 8 – 10

NOTE: WE SERVE THIS AS AN ACCOMPANIMENT TO LAMB, BUT IT IS ALSO A DELICIOUS DIP FOR VEGETABLES AND PITA CHIPS OR BREAD.

Grandma Logeman's Date Pudding

1 cup flour	1 cup brown sugar
1 cup sugar	2 cups hot water
1 teaspoon baking powder	1 tablespoon butter
1 cup dates, chopped	1 teaspoon vanilla
1 cup pecans or walnuts, chopped	Whipped cream or vanilla ice cream
½ cup milk	(optional)

Preheat oven to 350 degrees.

Grease a 9 x 9-inch pan or deep 9-inch pie plate. In a medium-size bowl, mix the flour, sugar, baking powder, dates, nuts and milk. This will be a very thick batter. Pour and spread into prepared pan. In another medium-size bowl, mix the brown sugar, hot water, butter and vanilla until the butter melts. Pour this over the batter in the pan and place on a baking sheet. Bake 45 minutes to 1 hour or until the top is nicely browned and bubbling. Let set 15 minutes. Serve warm with vanilla ice cream or whipped cream.

Serves 8 – 10

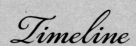

Timeline

1 WEEK AHEAD
- Shop for non-perishable groceries
- Order turkey
- Order lamb chops
- Order oysters

2 DAYS AHEAD
- Prepare your holiday table with platters and serving pieces
- Pick up turkey
- Make the salt rub
- Make the Tarator

1 DAY AHEAD
- Shop for last-minute groceries
- Pick up lamb chops
- Pick up oysters
- Rub the turkey with the salt mixture and refrigerate
- Grind the cranberries and add the sugar for the Laird Cranberry Salad
- Whip the cream and add the marshmallows for the Laird Cranberry Salad
- Make the Cranberry Sauce; refrigerate
- Chop the carrots, celery and onions for the Turkey
- Set up the bar
- Make bar garnishes

MORNING OF THE PARTY
- Chop the apples and oranges for the Turkey
- Prepare and cook the turkey
- Make the Corn Pudding and refrigerate until baking
- Make the Zelnik and refrigerate until baking

2 HOURS AHEAD
- Take out the milk and half & half to get to room temperature
- Finish making the Laird Cranberry Salad; refrigerate
- Make the Date Pudding; keep at room temperature; Bake 1 hour before you are ready for dessert

1 HOUR AHEAD
- Make the Gravy; keep warm
- Prep the Lamb Chops; keep at room temperature until grilling
- Bake the Corn Pudding
- Bake the Zelnik
- Bake the Date Pudding
- Make the Oyster Stew
- Plate the Tarator
- Plate the Laird Cranberry Salad and sprinkle with remaining slivered almonds

JUST BEFORE THE PARTY
- Set out all food items
- Grill the Lamb Chops
- Check bar; put ice in bucket; set out garnishes

Shopping List

Oysters, 2 quarts + 1 pint raw
Whole milk (½ gallon) plus
   1 ½ cups to make all recipes
Half & half, 1 quart
Oyster crackers
Greek-style yogurt, 5 cups
English cucumber, 1
Garlic, 1 bulb
Creamed corn, 1 15-ounce can
Eggs, 1 dozen
Cranberries, fresh, 2
   12-ounce bags
Heavy whipping cream, 1 pint
Mini marshmallows,
   10.5 ounce bag
Crushed pineapple,
   1 8-ounce can
Slivered almonds, 1 cup
Feta cheese, 11 ounces
   (we prefer Bulgarian feta)
Frozen spinach, 8 ounces
Phyllo dough, 1 package,
   found in the frozen
   dessert area
French cut lamb chops, 25
Oven roasting bag
Turkey, 14-16 pound
Carrots, 6 large
Celery stalks, 6
Onions, 3
Granny Smith apples, 2
Apple, red, 1
Oranges, 3
Lemons, 2
Turkey or chicken stock
   or broth, 3 ½ cups
Dates, 1 cup
Pecans or walnuts, 1 cup
Whipped cream or
   vanilla ice cream (optional)
Fetzer Riesling
Korbel champagne
Chambord liqueur
Old Forester bourbon
Jack Daniel's Tennessee
   Whiskey
Dumante pistachio nut
   liqueur

**ALSO BUY, IF NOT
IN YOUR PANTRY**

Unsalted butter
Celery seed
Worcestershire sauce
Kosher salt
Paprika
Hot sauce
Dried dill
Flour
Sugar
Brown Sugar
Vegetable oil
Baking soda
Baking powder
Olive oil
Greek seasoning
Dried rosemary
Dried rubbed sage
Dried thyme
Dried parsley
Bay leaves
Vanilla extract
Cloves
Cinnamon
Maple syrup
Roasting pan

Holiday

The holiday season means parties galore, with frequent entertaining and gatherings with family, friends and co-workers. The season can be full of stress due to busy schedules and the pressure of making sure everything is perfect. Take heart! There are simple ways to take the fear out of holiday entertaining. The secret lies in proper and efficient planning. A well-prepared plan eliminates stress and allows you to enjoy your party as much as your guests. Along with a pre-plan, make a checklist of activities well ahead of your event. This enables you to get organized and spread the workload over many days. You will feel a sense of accomplishment as you check off your tasks as the party date gets closer.

Holiday entertaining ranges from the very elegant to the comfortably casual. Depending on how you present and serve your dishes, this holiday menu will work for any style that suits you. Many people love the warmth of an informal setting, so do not feel pressure to make your table look like a magazine cover.

MENU

HOLIDAY CRAB AND CRACKERS

ASPARAGUS SPEARS WITH ASIAN DIPPING SAUCE

JACK SWEET POTATOES

MASHED POTATOES WITH GOAT CHEESE AND SAGE

POACHED SALMON WITH CUCUMBER SCALES

TENDERLOIN OF BEEF WITH BOURBON AU JUS AND HORSERADISH CREAM

POACHED PEARS IN RED WINE

HOLIDAY CRANTINI MARTINI

APPLES AND CINNAMON-INFUSED BOURBON

Holiday Hints and Tips

INVITATIONS

Due to this hectic time of year, invitations for holiday parties should go out 3 – 4 weeks before the event so your guests can be sure to put the date in their calendar.

For more formal parties, invitations can be purchased from a variety of stores, then personalized with your party information and mailed. Another option is to buy them online from a variety of websites.

For less formal events and to save money, you can send free online invitations from a variety of websites. Guests respond via email letting you know if they are "able to attend," "not able to attend" or "might attend." The host receives a quick response and can see at a glance how many people have responded and their status.

PARTY FAVORS

Guests love to leave with a little something to remember the evening. Place a basket near the door with your party favors so you will remember to give them to your guests on their way out. Here are a few suggestions:

- Put a couple handfuls of raw chestnuts (purchased at your local grocer at holiday time) in a small brown lunch bag, along with a slip of paper with directions on how to roast them.

  > "Roasted Chestnuts – Make a large "x" in each chestnut with a sharp paring knife, cutting through its shell. Roast the chestnuts in a 400-degree oven for 15 – 20 minutes, or until they are tender and the shells come off easily. Peel and enjoy. Happy Holidays."

- Individually-packaged holiday ornaments.
- Bake or purchase holiday cookies; wrap them in clear cellophane; tie with a festive bow.
- Bake or purchase glazed nuts; put them in mini-holiday-themed tins.

TABLE SETTING

A few days before the party, prepare your holiday buffet table. Take out the serving platters you plan to use and label each with the item you plan to serve. Determine where each will be placed and set out the necessary serving pieces.

Holiday Crantini Martini

3 ounces Finlandia cranberry vodka
6 ounces cranberry juice

1 ounce sweet and sour mix

FOR TWO COCKTAILS

In a shaker with ice, add the vodka, cranberry juice and sweet and sour. Strain into sugar-rimmed martini glasses and garnish with rosemary spears of fresh cranberries.

TO MAKE BY THE PITCHER

Use the ratio of 1 part vodka, 2 parts cranberry juice and ½ part sweet and sour. Combine in a pitcher, then shake with ice to make individual cocktails.

ALCOHOL-FREE

For an alcohol-free version, omit the vodka and replace it with club soda. Stir and pour into a martini glass.

Apples and Cinnamon-Infused Bourbon

1 liter Woodford Reserve bourbon	4 cinnamon sticks
5 ounces dried apples	

Pour all of the bourbon into a large pitcher. Into the now-empty bottle of bourbon, add the dried apples and cinnamon sticks. Carefully pour back enough bourbon to fill the bottle. Cap and let infuse for a minimum of three days.

The infused bourbon is great on its own, served neat in a glass or shaken with ice and strained into small martini glasses.

OTHER IDEAS
- Make several bottles and give them as holiday gifts, with the recipe attached and serving ideas
- Mix the infused bourbon with apple cider for a refreshing cocktail on ice
- Heat and serve it as a hot toddy and top with whipped cream
- For alternative flavors, the same process can be used with dried figs or dried peaches and a vanilla bean

Holiday Crab and Crackers

1½ pounds crab meat or imitation crab meat	Black pepper
8 ounces cream cheese	Cocktail sauce
4 drops Worcestershire sauce	Capers
Seasoned salt	Butter crackers

Whip cream cheese until it is very light and fluffy. Add the Worcestershire sauce to the cream cheese and a few shakes of seasoned salt and ground pepper to taste. In a large bowl, break the crab apart, still leaving some large chunks. Add spoonfuls of the cream cheese mixture until there is just enough to hold the crab together. Form crab mixture into a dome on a serving platter. Drizzle the cocktail sauce over the top. Sprinkle with capers. Serve with butter crackers.

Serves 12 – 15

NOTE: IF USING FRESH CRAB, MAKE SURE THE CRAB IS CLEAN AND FREE OF ALL SHELLS.

Asparagus Spears with Asian Dipping Sauce

2 pounds asparagus spears	1 teaspoon sesame oil
⅔ cup mayonnaise	1 orange
2 tablespoons soy sauce	

ASPARAGUS

Prepare a large bowl of cold water with ice. Pour 1 inch of water into a large frying pan and bring to a boil. Add the asparagus, return to a boil and cook until the asparagus is bright green and just tender, about 2 minutes. Plunge the asparagus into the cold water to stop the cooking process. When cool, drain well and pat dry. Refrigerate until ready to serve. Can be made earlier in the day.

SAUCE

In a small bowl, combine the mayonnaise, soy sauce and sesame oil. Grate the zest of the whole orange into the sauce, then cut the orange in half and squeeze in the juice, making sure to strain out the seeds. Combine well. Can be made a day ahead of time.

TO SERVE

Spoon the dipping sauce into a small bowl. Place the bowl in the middle of a round platter and fan the asparagus around it on the platter.

Serves 8 – 12

NOTE: TO MAKE THE ASPARAGUS MORE TENDER, BREAK OFF THE WOODY STEMS AND PEEL, USING A VEGETABLE PEELER TO EXPOSE THE BOTTOM HALF OF THE SPEAR. BE CAREFUL NOT TO OVERCOOK THE ASPARAGUS AS IT WILL BECOME LIMP AND DIFFICULT TO PICK UP AND DIP INTO THE SAUCE.

Jack Sweet Potatoes

3 29-ounce cans sweet potatoes	½ cup unsalted butter
1 cup brown sugar	½ teaspoon vanilla extract
⅓ cup Jack Daniel's Tennessee Whiskey	2 cups chopped pecans

Preheat oven to 350 degrees.

Heat the sweet potatoes in a large sauce pan, over medium heat. Drain off some of the liquid and mash the potatoes. Add the brown sugar, Jack Daniel's, butter and vanilla. Pour into 2-quart shallow baking dish. Sprinkle with pecans. Bake uncovered for 30 minutes, or until pecans are golden.

Serves 8 – 10

Mashed Potatoes with Goat Cheese and Sage

1 pound Yukon Gold potatoes, peeled and cut into 1-inch cubes	3 tablespoons butter
1 pound Idaho potatoes, peeled and cut into 1-inch cubes	3 teaspoons fresh sage, chopped
	Fresh sage sprigs, for garnish
5 ounces goat cheese, softened	Kosher salt
¼ cup milk, possibly a little more	Black pepper

In a large saucepan, boil the potatoes in salted water until tender, about 12 minutes. Drain well. Return potatoes to the same pan. Add the goat cheese, milk and butter. Mash until smooth. Add more milk to achieve desired consistency. Stir in chopped sage. Season to taste with salt and pepper. Garnish serving bowl or individual plates with fresh sage sprigs.

Serves 8 – 10

Poached Salmon with Cucumber Scales

1 3-4-pound top half of salmon, skin removed	¼ onion, sliced
Water	8 dill sprigs, 3 reserved for garnish
1 lemon, juiced	5 flat-leaf parsley sprigs
Black pepper	½ cup white wine
4 whole cloves	Spray oil

Combine the water, lemon juice, pepper, cloves, onion, dill, parsley and wine in the bottom of a fish poacher. Liquid should just reach the bottom of the poaching rack. Place the fish poacher on the stovetop covering 2 burners. Bring to a boil. Coat the rack with spray oil. Place the salmon on the rack, skin side down, cover. Poach for approximately 10 minutes per inch of thickness of salmon. An instant read thermometer should read 140 degrees in the thickest part. Salmon can be served by sprinkling with pepper and snipped dill or decorated (below).

Serves 10 – 12

NOTE: A FISH POACHER IS IDEAL FOR THIS RECIPE, BUT A LARGE DEEP ROASTING PAN COVERED WITH HEAVY-DUTY FOIL CAN BE USED INSTEAD. SALMON CAN BE POACHED THE DAY BEFORE AND STORED IN THE REFRIGERATOR OVERNIGHT UNDECORATED.

TO DECORATE THE SALMON

1 English seedless cucumber, sliced very thin	Black pepper
1½ cups sour cream	5 dill sprigs

When the salmon has cooled, sprinkle with black pepper. Snip fresh dill sprigs over the salmon, making sure to cover the whole fish lightly. With a knife, spread sour cream over the fish, just enough to cover. Starting at the tail end, layer cucumber slices, slightly overlapping to appear like scales. Repeat until entire fish is coated. Place on platter. Garnish with a dill sprig where the fin would naturally appear.

Tenderloin of Beef with Bourbon Au Jus and Horseradish Cream

5-pound beef tenderloin	1½ cups Italian salad dressing
(approximately ⅓ pound per person)	1 teaspoon soy sauce

In a large zip-top plastic bag, add the Italian dressing and soy sauce. Mix to combine. Add the beef tenderloin and seal. Marinate overnight in the refrigerator, turning occasionally to make sure it is evenly coated.

Preheat oven to 500 degrees.

Place tenderloin on roasting rack in a roasting pan. Do not cover or baste. Reduce the heat immediately to 400 degrees and bake for 30 minutes (for a 5-pound tenderloin) or until desired temperature is reached. A filet is usually cooked rare when the internal temperature reaches 125 degrees. It will rise at least another 10 degrees to 135 for medium rare. Let it rest for 10 minutes, then slice and serve.

Serves 12 – 15

NOTE: ASK YOUR BUTCHER TO TRIM AND TIE YOUR TENDERLOIN. REMOVE TENDERLOIN FROM THE REFRIGERATOR 1 HOUR BEFORE COOKING TO ALLOW IT TO COME TO ROOM TEMPERATURE.

Au Jus

1 10.5-ounce can of beef broth	¼ cup unsalted butter
4 cloves garlic	¼ cup Woodford Reserve bourbon

Slowly simmer the beef broth and garlic cloves for approximately 15 minutes. When the tenderloin comes out of the oven, add the butter and bourbon to the *au jus*. Pour over the tenderloin and let it rest before slicing. You may want to reserve some of the *au jus* to pour over individual slices on each plate.

Horseradish Cream

1 cup sour cream	Black pepper
2 tablespoons horseradish	Kosher salt

In a small bowl, combine the sour cream and horseradish. Add the salt and pepper to taste.

Poached Pears in Red Wine

8 medium-size pears, very firm

1 cup sugar

2 cups dry red wine, such as
   Fetzer cabernet sauvignon

4 cloves

1 teaspoon vanilla extract

Carefully peel the pears, retaining the stem. Cut a small slice off the bottom of each pear so they stand upright.

In a saucepan large enough to fit the pears lying on their side, add the sugar, red wine, cloves and vanilla. Bring to a boil. Put the pears on their side in the pan and simmer, covered, for 25 - 30 minutes, turning over after 15 minutes. Check for doneness by inserting a small sharp knife into the bottom of each pear. The knife should glide in easily. Remove the pears and stand in a dish large enough for an oversized spoon to fit. Reduce the liquid in the pan to a syrup. It will start to foam when ready. Drizzle the syrup over pears. Baste often with the syrup in the bottom of the dish until a rich, glossy red color develops.

Serves 8

NOTE: THE PEARS SHOULD BE VERY FIRM, BARELY YIELDING TO THE TOUCH. IF THEY ARE TOO RIPE, THEY WILL GET TOO SOFT DURING THE POACHING PROCESS.

Timeline

1 WEEK AHEAD
- Shop for non-perishable groceries
- Order beef tenderloin
- Order salmon
- Shop for party favors
- Make the Apples and Cinnamon-Infused Bourbon

2 DAYS AHEAD
- Prepare your holiday table with platters and serving pieces
- Prepare party favors

1 DAY AHEAD
- Shop for last-minute groceries
- Pick up beef tenderloin
- Pick up salmon
- Make the Holiday Crab and Crackers
- Make the Asian Dipping Sauce
- Marinate the beef tenderloin
- Make the Jack Sweet Potatoes
- Make the Mashed Potatoes with Goat Cheese and Sage
- Make the Horseradish Cream
- Poach the salmon
- Make pitchers of the Holiday Crantini
- Make the rosemary and cranberry garnishes
- Set up the bar
- Make bar garnishes

MORNING OF THE PARTY
- Steam the asparagus
- Make the Bourbon Au Jus
- Take out, bake and slice the beef tenderloin if serving at room temperature

2 HOURS AHEAD
- Decorate the salmon; keep cold until serving
- Make the Poached Pears in Red Wine; continue basting until serving

1 HOUR AHEAD
- Plate the Holiday Crab and Crackers; finish with cocktail sauce and capers
- Plate the Asparagus Spears with Asian Dipping Sauce
- Plate the Beef Tenderloin (serve at room temperature)
- Heat the Jack Sweet Potatoes; keep warm
- Heat the Mashed Potatoes with Goat Cheese and Sage; keep warm
- Plate the Poached Pears in Red Wine
- Put rolls in basket with napkin

JUST BEFORE THE PARTY
- Set out all food items
- Check bar; fill ice buckets; set out garnishes

Shopping List

Asparagus spears, 2 pounds

Orange, 1

1½ pounds crab meat or
   imitation crab meat

Cream cheese, 8 ounces

Cocktail sauce

Capers

Butter crackers

Sweet potatoes,
   3 29-ounce cans

Jack Daniel's
   Tennessee Whiskey

Chopped pecans, 2 cups

Yukon Gold potatoes, 1 pound

Idaho potatoes, 1 pound

Goat cheese, 5 ounces

Sage, 1 bunch

Salmon, 1 3-4-pound,
   top half, skin removed

Lemon, 1

Whole cloves

Onion, 1

Dill, 1 bunch

Flat-leaf parsley, 1 bunch

Chardonnay

English seedless cucumber, 1

Sour cream

Horseradish

Beef tenderloin
   (approximately ⅓ pound
   per person)

Italian salad dressing

Beef broth, 1 10.5-ounce can

Garlic, 1 bulb

Woodford Reserve bourbon

Dried apples, 5 ounces

Rolls, 12

Pears, very firm

Fetzer cabernet sauvignon

Finlandia cranberry vodka

Cranberry juice

Sweet and sour mix

Cranberries, 1 bag, fresh

Fresh Rosemary, 2 bunches

**ALSO BUY, IF NOT
IN YOUR PANTRY**

Kosher salt

Black pepper

Sugar

Worcestershire sauce

Mayonnaise

Soy sauce

Sesame oil

Spray oil

Brown sugar

Milk

Vanilla extract

Unsalted butter

Cinnamon sticks

Seasoned salt

New Year's Eve

Ring in the New Year by hosting your own New Year's Eve party but don't drop the ball. Save that for TV!

New Year's Eve is synonymous with champagne. More than half of all champagne sales occur just a few days prior to New Year's Eve. Honestly, we should enjoy champagne year round, and not save it just for this occasion or special celebrations. As a matter of fact, champagne pairs well with just about every food combination so consider champagne as your dinner accompaniment along with or instead of wine.

Since many are intimidated with opening a bottle of champagne due to the pressure (99 pounds per square inch, 3 times that of a car tire), I have included five easy steps so you can save it for sipping and not spraying.

FIVE EASY STEPS TO OPENING A CHAMPAGNE BOTTLE JUST LIKE THE PROFESSIONALS

1. Chill the bottle for at least 4 hours in the refrigerator.
2. Remove the foil cap covering the top of the bottle, exposing the wire hood.
3. Undo the wire hood with 6 half-turns of the knob (many do not know this, but all wire hoods have 6 half-turns).
4. Hold the bottle at a 45° angle, with a towel in hand. Grasp the cork tightly and slowly twist the bottle with your other hand (the big secret here is you twist the bottle, not the cork).
5. Ease the cork off the bottle, letting out a small sigh, while keeping the bottle at a 45° angle for a moment (this lets the air in and helps keep the foam from overflowing).

TIPS FOR YOUR NEW YEARS EVE PARTY

- Decorate your party area with horns, hats, streamers, confetti and other New Year's Eve festive décor.
- Have fun board or card games on hand to play, while waiting to ring in the New Year.
- A champagne punch is perfect for your signature cocktail. Be sure to save some so you have plenty for your champagne toast at midnight.

- Offer alcohol-free sparkling drinks made with lemon-lime or club soda.
- Start your food presentations with items that need to be consumed immediately. This includes fresh oysters, shrimp and other seafood items. Next, set out plenty of heavy appetizers that will last well into the next year.
- Keep an eye on the clock to make sure your food and drinks are well-spaced throughout the night, including putting out more alcohol-free beverages later in the evening.
- Be a responsible host and have cab vouchers or designated drivers available for anyone who may have partied a little too much.

BAN THE FLUTE

Note on glassware: There have been many discussions surrounding the type of glassware to use for champagne. Originally the coupe or saucer-style glass was used. After many years it was then believed the wide opening would lead to too many bubbles escaping, making the champagne flat. Enter the flute, a long narrow glass which holds very little champagne. In my book, this is a bad glass and should be banned. What glass to use? A white wine glass is perfect to multi-task for this job. It has a wider opening which is easy to pour into and drink from. It also allows plenty of space for added juices to make a flavorful champagne cocktail. The white wine glass is much more stable than the flute and easier to clean. It does not make sense to start a whole new collection of glasses just for champagne when our white wine glass can answer the call of the bubbles.

Champagne Punch

2 750-ml bottles Korbel Brut champagne | Dash of bitters
2 tablespoons superfine sugar | 1 pint fresh raspberries
½ lime, juiced

Combine all ingredients in a punch bowl and add a block of ice. Serve immediately.

Serves 8 – 10

Raw Oysters

Buy raw oysters from your favorite fishmonger or nearby seafood restaurant. Make sure they shuck the oysters for you so you only need to place them on a bed of crushed ice just before your guests arrive. Serve with lemon wedges, hot sauce and horseradish on the side, so your guests can garnish them as they like. Plan on 2 – 3 oysters per person.

Shrimp Cocktail

You can either poach your own shrimp or buy a bag of frozen, jumbo-size shrimp, already cooked (peeled, cleaned and deveined) with the tail on. Defrost the frozen shrimp in your refrigerator overnight, then rinse with cold water and a squeeze of lemon. Let dry in your refrigerator. Just before serving, place a zip-top plastic bag with crushed ice on your platter, cover with leafy lettuce, then arrange your shrimp on top. Sprinkle with your favorite seafood seasoning and serve with lemon wedges and cocktail sauce. For those who like it spicy, serve an additional cocktail sauce with lots of added horseradish. This will turn it a pink color. Plan on 2 – 3 shrimp per person.

Ahi and Salmon Spoons

½ pound sushi-grade ahi tuna, diced	½ pound sushi-grade salmon, diced

FOR THE SAUCE

1 tablespoon soy sauce	½ teaspoon grated fresh ginger
1 tablespoon rice wine vinegar	Black sesame seeds
1 teaspoon sesame oil	White sesame seeds
½ tablespoon sugar	Rice crackers (optional)
½ teaspoon wasabi paste	

In a small bowl, combine the soy sauce, rice wine vinegar, sesame oil, sugar, wasabi paste and ginger. In a separate small bowl, combine the ahi tuna with ½ of the sauce. In another small bowl, combine the salmon with the remaining ½ of the sauce. Place a bite-size amount on spoons or rice crackers, sprinkle with sesame seeds and serve immediately.

Makes 32 bite-size servings

Caviar Pie

8 eggs, hard-boiled, finely chopped

4 tablespoons unsalted butter
   (½ stick), melted

2 tablespoons chives, finely chopped

1 teaspoon celery salt

1 teaspoon dry mustard

1 teaspoon salt

1 teaspoon black pepper

1 cup Greek or plain yogurt

1 4-ounce jar black or red caviar, rinsed
   and well-drained

Whole wheat bread, very thin, crusts cut off

Water crackers (optional)

Finely chop the hard-boiled eggs by hand or in a food processor. In a medium-size bowl, mix the eggs, butter, chives, celery salt, dry mustard, salt and pepper. Rinse a 9-inch glass pie plate in cold water and press egg mixture into it to form a crust. Cover the eggs with a thick layer of yogurt. Freeze for 1 hour. Remove from freezer and top with the caviar. Refrigerate until serving time. Serve with toast points or water crackers.

Serves 8 – 10

Black-Eyed Pea Dip

2 15½-ounce cans black-eyed peas, drained	4 cloves garlic, crushed
1 cup red onion, diced	½ cup Italian salad dressing
1 cup red pepper, diced	1 tablespoon black pepper
1 cup green pepper, diced	2 tablespoons cilantro, chopped
1 jalapeño pepper, seeds and ribs removed, diced	Pita chips

In a medium-size bowl, combine the black-eyed peas, red onion, red pepper, green pepper, jalapeño, garlic, Italian dressing and black pepper. Refrigerate overnight. Take out 30 minutes before serving and add the cilantro. Serve with pita chips.

Serves 8 – 10

Toasted Chickpeas and Pistachios

2 15½-ounce cans chickpeas, drained	1 teaspoon ground ginger
¼ cup vegetable oil	1 teaspoon ground coriander
1 teaspoon Kosher salt	½ teaspoon cayenne pepper
1 teaspoon ground cumin	1½ cups raw pistachio nuts, shelled
1 teaspoon black pepper	2 teaspoons fresh thyme leaves

Preheat oven to 400 degrees.

In a medium-size bowl, toss the chickpeas with the vegetable oil, salt, cumin, black pepper, ginger, coriander and cayenne pepper. Spread in an even layer on a rimmed baking sheet and bake for 15 minutes, stirring after 8 minutes with a spatula. Remove from the oven and stir in pistachio nuts and thyme. Return to the oven and bake for an additional 10 minutes. Transfer the mixture into a serving dish and serve warm.

Serves 8 – 10

Bourbon Bacon Toasts

1 pound bacon	2 tablespoons Woodford Reserve bourbon
1 loaf whole wheat bread	2 tablespoons chives, finely chopped
1 jar mango chutney	

Preheat broiler to high.

Cook bacon until crisp. Chop into fine pieces and place on a plate. Using a cookie cutter or the top of a jar, stamp out 1½-inch bread rounds. You can usually get 3 rounds per slice of bread. In a small bowl, mix the mango chutney and bourbon (you may want to heat the chutney slightly in the microwave so it incorporates easier). Spread a generous amount of the chutney mixture on a bread round, then dip it in the bacon pieces so they stick to the bread. Repeat the steps for each bread round. Just before serving, heat under the broiler to further crisp the bacon. Sprinkle with chopped chives and serve immediately.

Serves 8 – 10

NOTE: THE TOASTS CAN BE MADE ONE DAY AHEAD AND STORED IN THE REFRIGERATOR UNTIL READY TO BROIL AND SERVE.

Prosciutto-Wrapped Figs

20 fresh figs	Toothpicks
4 ounces blue cheese	Olive oil
10 slices prosciutto, halved lengthwise	Pepper

Preheat oven to 400 degrees.

Cut the figs partially in half. Place a pea-size ball of blue cheese inside each fig and pinch closed. Wrap each fig with a slice of prosciutto and secure with a toothpick. Brush each bundle with a small amount of olive oil and sprinkle with pepper. Bake for 10 minutes. Serve warm or at room temperature.

Serves 8 – 10

Two-Bite Beef Tenderloin Sliders

If you do not have time to cook your own beef tenderloin, pick it up already cooked from your favorite market or the prepared food area of your local grocery store and have it sliced thick (¼-inch). Place one piece of beef on a "slider" or mini hamburger bun and add a lettuce leaf. Serve with Dijon mustard and steak sauce on the side. Plan on 1 – 2 sandwiches per person.

Frozen Banana Pops

1 cup bittersweet chocolate chips	½ cup walnuts, crushed and toasted
½ tablespoon vegetable oil	½ cup shredded coconut, toasted
1 Heath bar, crushed	3 bananas, peeled and cut into ½-inch slices
1 Butterfinger bar, crushed	30 skewers

Line baking sheet with foil.

Melt chocolate and oil in a small saucepan over low heat. Take off the heat and cool for 10 minutes. Place each topping in a small bowl. Drop a piece of banana into the chocolate and remove using toothpicks, shaking off any excess chocolate. Drop into topping and coat completely. Remove and place on a baking sheet. Poke a skewer in the center. Repeat with remaining bananas, chocolate and toppings. Freeze until firm, a minimum of 4 hours or overnight. Take out of the freezer, arrange on your platter and serve.

Serves 8 – 10

NOTE: USE YOUR FAVORITE CANDY OR NUT TOPPINGS.

Timeline

1 WEEK AHEAD
- Shop for non-perishable groceries
- Shop for party favors

3 DAYS AHEAD
- Prepare your table with platters, serving pieces and decorations
- Order raw oysters
- Order beef tenderloin slices
- Order sushi-grade ahi tuna
- Order sushi-grade salmon
- Set out card and board games

1 DAY AHEAD
- Shop for last-minute groceries
- Pick up beef tenderloin slices
- Make the sauce for the Ahi Tuna and Salmon Spoons
- Put the frozen shrimp in refrigerator to thaw
- Wash leafy lettuce and other fresh herbs
- Make or buy a bag of crushed ice, keep in freezer
- Make the Prosciutto-Wrapped Figs
- Make the Black-Eyed Pea Dip
- Make the Bourbon Bacon Toasts
- Make the Frozen Banana Pops and set out when ready for dessert
- Set up the bar
- Make bar garnishes
- Slice lemons

MORNING OF THE PARTY
- Pick up oysters; keep on ice in refrigerator
- Pick up the ahi tuna and salmon; dice and refrigerate
- Make the Caviar Pie and toasts

2 HOURS AHEAD
- Rinse the shrimp and refrigerate until ready to serve
- Put cocktail sauce in a small bowl; make spicy cocktail sauce; refrigerate both
- Make the Two-Bite Beef Tenderloin Sliders; refrigerate

1 HOUR AHEAD
- Pour the sauce over the ahi tuna and salmon; plate and refrigerate
- Plate the Shrimp Cocktail and refrigerate
- Make the Toasted Chickpeas and Pistachios; leave at room temperature
- Plate the Black-Eyed Pea Dip; set out pita chips

JUST BEFORE THE PARTY
- Bake the Prosciutto-Wrapped Figs and plate
- Bake the Toasted Chickpeas and Pistachios and plate
- Broil the Bourbon Bacon Toasts, garnish with chives and plate
- Plate the Raw Oysters; set out lemon, hot sauce and horseradish
- Make the Easy Champagne Punch
- Set out all other food items
- Check bar; put ice in bucket; set out garnishes

Shopping List

Sushi-grade ahi tuna,
   ½ pound
Sushi-grade salmon, ½ pound
Rice wine vinegar
Sesame oil
Wasabi paste
Ginger, 1 knob
Black sesame seeds
White sesame seeds
Rice crackers (optional)
Frozen shrimp, cooked, 1
   2-pound bag, jumbo size
Cocktail sauce
Lemons, 3
Horseradish (optional)
Leafy lettuce, 1 head
Raw oysters, 2 dozen
Fresh figs, 20
Blue cheese, 4 ounces
Prosciutto, 10 slices
Toothpicks
Black-eyed peas,
   2 15½-ounce cans
Red onion, 1
Red pepper, 1
Green pepper, 1
Jalapeño, 1
Garlic, 1 bulb
Italian salad dressing
Cilantro, 1 bunch
Pita Chips
Eggs, 1 dozen
Chives, 1 bunch
Greek or plain yogurt, 1 cup
Black or red caviar,
   14-ounce jar
Whole wheat bread,
   very thin, 1 loaf
Water crackers (optional)
Chickpeas, 2 15½-ounce cans
Raw pistachio nuts, 1½ cups
Fresh thyme leaves, 1 bunch
Bacon, 1 pound
Whole wheat bread, 1 loaf
Mango chutney, 1 jar
Woodford Reserve bourbon

Beef tenderloin slices, 25
Mini or slider hamburger
   buns, 2 packages
Bittersweet chocolate chips,
   1 bag
Heath bar, 1
Butterfinger bar, 1
Walnuts, ½ cup
Shredded coconut, 1 bag
Bananas, 3
Korbel Brut champagne,
   2 750-ml bottles
Lime, 1
Fresh raspberries, 1 pint

ALSO BUY, IF NOT IN YOUR PANTRY

Soy sauce
Sugar
Olive oil
Black pepper
Unsalted butter
Celery salt
Dry mustard
Kosher salt
Ground cumin
Ground ginger
Ground coriander
Cayenne pepper
Dijon mustard
Steak sauce
Hot sauce
Zip-top plastic bags,
   1-gallon size
Vegetable oil
Skewers, 30
Superfine sugar
Bitters
Toothpicks

Home Bar

Home Bar

The bar is a very important component to entertaining. There are a few must-have tools, spirits, mixers, condiments and glassware that make a home bar able to satisfy any guest. Start with the basics and build as you go. Always remember to be a responsible host and offer plenty of alcohol-free choices.

BAR TOOLS

- Cobbler shaker (three pieces: tin, top with strainer and cap)
- Boston shaker (two pieces: mixing glass and tin)
- Good insulated ice bucket that doesn't sweat when filled with ice
- Ice scoop or tongs
- Sharp knife to cut fruit
- Fruit reamer
- Cocktail spoon
- Juicer
- Muddler
- Hawthorn and Julep strainers (Hawthorn holds back the ice and larger ingredients, the Julep will help with any pulp or other materials)
- Jiggers – 1 with 1-and 2-ounce cups, 1 with ¾-and 1½-ounce cups
- Microplane for zesting fruit and shaving chocolate and nutmeg
- Wine key or opener
- Channel knife for making twists
- Mixing glass
- Cutting board

SPIRITS CHECKLIST

- Vodka
- Rum
- Tequila
- Gin
- Tennessee Whiskey
- Bourbon
- Brandy
- Triple sec or orange liqueur
- Raspberry liqueur

MIXER CHECKLIST

- Lemon juice (fresh)
- Lime juice (fresh)
- Sweetened lime juice
- Lemon-lime soda
- Cola
- Club soda
- Tonic water
- Orange juice
- Tomato juice
- Pineapple juice
- Grapefruit juice
- Cranberry juice

FUNDAMENTAL CONDIMENT CHECKLIST

- Bitters (regular and orange)
- Grenadine syrup
- Tabasco
- Superfine sugar
- Cream (heavy and light)
- Simple syrup

GARNISH CHECKLIST

- Cocktail olives
- Cocktail onions
- Limes
- Lemons
- Maraschino cherries
- Strawberries

GLASSWARE

- Three types will satisfy most cocktails. Look for glassware that is simple in shape, easy to handle and with a thin lip or rim.
- Rocks or bucket glass
- Collins or tall
- Martini or cocktail

COCKTAILS

- Cocktails are the life of the party. A well-made drink highlights the spirit, while balancing other flavors.
- The original cocktails were quite simple. In 1806, a newspaper article described them as a spirit of any kind, water, sugar and bitters.
- Many of the originals have stood the test of time like the Manhattan and the Daiquiri.
- The Manhattan is whiskey, sweet vermouth and bitters.
- The classic Daiquiri is rum, lime juice and simple syrup.
- Today there are many recipes and new concoctions for cocktails with a vast array of flavors and spices. Bartenders are becoming bar chefs as they experiment with new ingredients, herbs and spices. Like cooking, I invite you to experiment with new flavors and spirits at home as well. Here are a few tips on making and designing cocktails.

COCKTAIL TIPS

- Always measure each ingredient.
- Always use fresh ingredients, when possible.
- Unless a recipe calls for crushed ice, always use large cubes of fresh, solid ice so your cocktail will not become overly diluted.
- If a recipe calls for crushed ice, place the large cubes in a clean bar towel, wrap and crush by knocking with a rolling pin or mallet.
- Never re-use ice in a cocktail shaker.
- Fill ice cube trays with bottled or filtered water to avoid "off" flavors.
- When serving a drink over ice, always fill the glass with ice to the top, then fill with the chilled cocktail from a shaker or glass.
- When a recipe calls for mixing champagnes with liqueurs such as a Kir Royal (Korbel champagne and Chambord liqueur) pour the champagne first, then add your liqueur to help blend as the liqueurs are heavier in density.
- Always fill your shaker two-thirds full of ice and shake for a good 25 seconds.
- Never shake carbonated beverages.
- Always garnish your cocktails.
- When making pitcher drinks or bulk recipes, add 4-8 ounces of water to allow for the dilution that happens when shaking or stirring individual drinks with ice.

INDEX